Belief

BELIEF

—

Gianni Vattimo

Translated by
Luca D'Isanto and David Webb

Stanford University Press
Stanford, California
1999

Stanford University Press
Stanford, California
© 1996 Garzanti Editore
© 1999 Polity Press for translation
Originally published as *Credere di Credere* in Italy
  by Garzanti Editore, 1996
Originating publisher of English edition:
  Polity Press in association with Blackwell Publishers Ltd
First published in the U.S.A. by Stanford University
  Press, 1999
Published with the assistance of the Italian Ministry
  of Foreign Affairs
Printed in Great Britain
Cloth ISBN 0–8047–3918–8
Paper ISBN 0–8047–3919–6
LC 99–72783
This book is printed on acid-free paper.

Contents

Introduction

Luca D'Isanto

Over the last decade, Gianni Vattimo has helped in bringing about a decisive shift in the field of hermeneutical philosophy, that is, of interpretation theory. Vattimo has followed Heidegger and Nietzsche in underscoring the impossibility of seeking universal and stable principles or values in philosophy. Heidegger and Nietzsche observed that since philosophical questions have changed dramatically with the coming and going of different historical generations of philosophers, philosophy belongs to the horizon of its historical epoch. Therefore, the traditional questions of philosophy (for example, about the nature of experience, freedom and the good life) cannot be answered by seeking an immutable order of things, but rather are provisional and valid only for a particular historically situated community.

Nietzsche speaks of 'nihilism' in order to give a name to the way in which nineteenth-century philosophy experiences the impossibility of finding a logical or epistemological access to universal, foundational knowledge. For Nietzsche, nihilism consists in the event of the death of God, the announcement that the world has become a *fable*. Since God was the most extreme hypothesis for a humanity in need of reassurance, the foundational principle placed above and

beyond contingent interpretations, this shift requires the
death of God. Nietzsche writes:

> The supreme values in whose service man should live,
> especially when they were hard on him and exacted a high
> price – these social values were erected over man to
> strengthen their voice, as if they were commands of God, as
> 'reality,' as true world, as a hope and future world. Now
> that the shabby origin of these values is becoming clear, the
> universe seems to have lost value, seems 'meaningless – but
> that is only a transitional stage'.[1]

In other words, Nietzsche believes that what we call the
'world' is not a reality which is independent of our own
historical schemes, but rather a game of interpretations. In
Vattimo's words: 'The images of the world we receive from
the media and the human sciences, albeit on different levels,
are not simply different interpretations of a reality that is
"given" regardless, but rather constitute the very objectivity
of the world.'[2] The fabulization of the world, of which
Nietzsche speaks, becomes understandable precisely in the
'communication societies' in which we live, and consists in
the weakening of the principle of reality in the world of
techno-science. Fabulization, understood as the weakening
of the principle of reality, consists in the recognition that the
world is increasingly identified with a proliferation of *Welt-
bilder*, of images of the world which give rise to conflict of
interpretation. The knowing subject can no longer secure
the object – that is, as an object of knowledge – because the
very limits between the subject and the object have become
opaque. The subject and the object have become hybrids of
each other. Indeed, both subject and object disappear from
the accounts of modern science:

[1] Nietzsche, *Will to Power* (New York: Vintage Books, 1968), 10.
[2] Vattimo, 'The Human Sciences and the Society of Communication', in *The
Transparent Society*, trans. David Webb (Cambridge: Polity Press, 1992), 24–5.

If the proliferation of images of the world entails that we lose our sense of reality, as the saying goes, perhaps it is not such a great loss after all. By a perverse kind of internal logic, the world of objects measured and manipulated by techno-science (the world of the real, according to metaphysics) has become the world of merchandise and images, the phantas-magoria of the mass media.[3]

The awareness that the world can no longer be thought of in terms of objectivity transforms and weakens the sense of reality. Is then every image of reality arbitrary? Certainly not, says Vattimo. Nietzsche's thesis concerning nihilism does not entail that every image of reality is arbitrary. Rather, it takes account of the fact that our 'image' no longer corresponds to the objectivity of the object, because the object itself has disappeared from our (scientific) view.

Heidegger speaks of nihilism, too. For him, nihilism means that what is constitutive of man – his Being – is concealed once metaphysics has taken its course and no longer provides the stable model of reality. The world of techno-science, the *Ge-Stell*, reduces Being to the realm of calculable and manipulable beings. The human being becomes merely the object of analysis, of the accumulation of detailed knowledge, thereby losing the distinction between historical being and objects. Nihilism is the process of the erosion of the essence of man, the concealment of the meaning of what is proper to the human being, of what it means 'to be' a human being. Hence, raising the question of Being, for Heidegger, has to do with recovering the freedom that pertains to the human being, the freedom of existence to project itself authentically into the future by affirming its own mortality and historicity.

Vattimo further elaborates Heidegger's and Nietzsche's conception of philosophy. He defines his project as a 'phil-

[3] Vattimo, *The Transparent Society*, 8.

osophy of actuality' that offers an analysis of the sense of existence in the technologically oriented postmodern society. Vattimo tries to disclose the sense of existence by seeking a 'logical thread' in the event of nihilism described by Nietzsche and Heidegger. For them, nihilism is a process of the progressive alienation of humanity in the epoch of techno-science, a process that renders many of the metaphysical issues raised by the philosophical tradition meaningless. Heidegger, though, ends up with a pessimistic attitude towards techno-science, one expressed in the famous posthumously published interview in *Der Spiegel* through the words 'Only a God can save us.'

Nietzsche's reaction to nihilism is more combative. Nietzsche makes a distinction between a reactive nihilism (one which sees the nullity of the world as a matter of oppression and pessimism), and an active nihilism, one which joyfully – that is, without resentment – embraces the nullity of the world and reinvents itself artistically.

Vattimo takes seriously Nietzsche's announcement of an active nihilism. However, he sees the necessity of interpreting nihilism from the perspective of Heidegger's question of Being. Thus he suggests that to celebrate Nietzsche's active nihilism we have to assume techno-science as the destiny of our culture, the effect of a common history. Heidegger, says Vattimo, 'teaches us that modernity is accomplished as nihilism, *Ge-stell*, the world of technological and scientific rationalization, the world of the conflict between the *Welt-bilder*. This is the world in which *Ereignis* "flashes", in which there is a chance to overcome metaphysics precisely because humanity and Being lose their metaphysical qualities, above all those of subject and object.'[4] This loss of the metaphysical qualities of subject and object, however, heralds the possi-

[4] Vattimo, 'Ethics of Communication, Ethics of Interpretation', in *The Transparent Society*, 115–16.

bility of emancipation precisely in the epoch of the triumph of technology, when the distance between the human subject and the objectivity of the world is placed in question. As Foucault has observed, modern technology increasingly concerns itself with the total control of every form of existence, with the seizure of every region of being. Even the subject falls into the totalizing grasp of the new technologies, thereby concealing or losing altogether what the metaphysical tradition called the free subject, that is, the subject as bearer of universal rights.[5]

Vattimo notes that if philosophers accept the stories that Nietzsche and Heidegger tell, they are confronted by two different problems. On the one hand, the philosopher can no longer appeal to universal knowledge to overcome alienation (that is, the fragmentation of existence into specialized sectors and languages). On the other, technology's greatest threat lies precisely in the possibility that it may achieve what metaphysics can no longer aspire to. It may bring together all the spheres of existence by submitting them to its total control. Vattimo argues that both instances reveal in a paradoxical way the hermeneutical vocation of philosophy, because each scenario requires the capacity of inhabiting worlds – or somehow mediating between them – whose meaning has become opaque.

For Vattimo, hermeneutical philosophy may indeed aspire to overcome the alienation of sense. It may do so by offering an interpretation of the present condition of fragmentation as coming from a common history, a common destiny. From this perspective, the sense of existence arises out of 'a' continuity with the historical transmission as well as with the present. Such a continuity, however, is not given once and for all; it is not an embodied set of truths valid for all

---

[5] Michel Foucault, *'Il faut défendre la société' Cours au Collège de France, 1976* (Paris: Gallimard Seuil, 1997), 241.

generations. On the contrary, sense, for Vattimo, discloses itself as a mobile horizon, as the crystallization of a 'provisional' horizon of understanding. Sense must be reconstructed again and again against the threat of fragmentation presented by the rationalization of the modern world.

If nihilism is understood as the destiny of our culture, then, it can be seen as 'an event which descends from the very logic of metaphysics; and to recognize it constitutes a real change within the history of metaphysics'.[6] To recognize the arrival of nihilism as a guest at our door – to use Nietzsche's expression – means to listen to the announcement of an event and to carry it to its logical conclusion. Vattimo observes that Nietzsche's thesis concerning the death of God is not intended as a metaphysical statement that might be demonstrated. On the contrary, it is the narration of an experience which is announced to others, so that they too may discover its truth for themselves, 'constituting on the basis of this a *we* to which and in the name of which the name of Nietzsche might speak'.[7] Thus the announcement of nihilism has ethical and political implications insofar as it calls for a community which will remain in the future, and, if realized, can find its truth in continuity with a common history.

For Vattimo, the most theoretically consistent way of putting forward Heidegger's and Nietzsche's project is to accept fully the linguistic turn, upon which a hermeneutical philosophy is premised. Using a Heideggerian terminology, Vattimo claims that Being is revealed as time-language. ' "Being is language" means that Being hands itself over in a diversified multiplicity of myths, narrations and language games that correspond to forms of life; "Being is time" '

---

[6] Vattimo, *Al di lá del soggetto: Nietzsche, Heidegger e l'ermeneutica* (Milan: Feltrinelli, 1981), 36.

[7] Vattimo, 'Metafisica, violenza, secolarizzazione', in *Filosofia 86*, ed. Gianni Vattimo (Milan: Laterza, 1987), 72.

means that Being hands itself over in forms that are never definitive, but always new, and by means of a flux of subsequent interpretations.'[8] Thus, Being coincides with the historical transmission of messages that unfold in time, and of which we can never have an exhaustive understanding. Our understanding is limited by our finitude, our linguistic horizons, which coincide with the historical-natural languages that make every experience of the world possible.

Vattimo has proposed to reorient hermeneutic philosophy in the direction of nihilism, renouncing the project of absolute knowledge or the search for foundational principles. Accordingly, hermeneutic philosophy must recognize that it is itself an interpretation, and not the description of how things really are 'out there'. Such a philosophy may even be able to defend the traditional claim to universality to which some hermeneutic philosophers have aspired, because it does not propose conclusive solutions *for the present*. This paradoxical form of universality lies in the coincidence between the logic of interpretation and the logic of nihilism, that is, the idea of an open configuration that is infinitely repeatable, 'which is able to refute itself, to correct itself and includes the possibility of its own nothingness'.[9] In other words, hermeneutics may be truthful precisely because it is aware of being merely a provisional – therefore never definitive, never ultimate – interpretation of the announcement that comes from the transmission of messages.

A philosophy of actuality, for Vattimo, aims to interpret the present condition of existence, the meaning of the subject in late modernity. The experience of the postmodern subject – he claims – resembles that of an 'interpreter' who

[8] Franca D'Agostini, 'Logica ermeneutica', in *Interpretazione ed emancipazione: studi in onore di Gianni Vattimo*, ed. Gianni Carchia and Maurizio Ferraris (Milan: Raffaele Cortina Editore, 1995), 174.
[9] Franca D'Agostini, *Analitici e continentali: guida alla filosofia degli ultimi trent'anni* (Milan: Raffaele Cortina, 1997), 148.

is not the author of his or her own text. In other words, there is an awareness of belonging to a chain of messages 'as a moment of a process, which can never come to closure, which includes and transcends them'.[10] Such a chain is discontinuous insofar as it is interrupted by the rhythm of mortal generations that come into being and then pass away. The chain of messages consists in the historical-natural languages that make every experience of the world possible. There is no established continuity between the various messages, nor any ultimate reference to a common universal essence under which they could be subsumed. How then does one find a sense, a sort of continuity with such a transmission? Vattimo argues that one may find a – provisional – sense by placing oneself (that is, by interpretative listening) within these messages (texts, cultures, myths), thus rescuing them from the dispersion of the present and taking responsibility for it.

Vattimo writes in this text that in the 1980s he began to see parallels between the kenotic messages of the gospel – the 'emptying out' of the divine into the human as a precondition for charity, as the word's etymology implies in the Christian tradition – and nihilistic philosophy. Kenosis here is understood as the hope for a peaceful humanity, but the analogy with nihilism does not imply, for Vattimo, a 'conversion' to Christianity. Indeed, Vattimo is suspicious of religious discourse about conversion which he sees as appealing to an authentic experience of the origin, the *arche*, to be secured and possessed by an act of thought. The logic of conversion may belong to the metaphysical heritage in two ways. First, it retains the idea of the origin that must be secured by thought, an act which is permeated by violence. Vattimo agrees with the idea Nietzsche expresses in the

---

[10] Vattimo, 'Nietzsche e il testo della metafisica (sulle recenti interpretazioni di Nietzsche in Francia)', in *Amicizie Stellare: Studi su Nietzsche*, ed. Alfredo Marini (Milan): Edizioni Unicopli, 1982), 326.

Genealogy of Morals, that metaphysics consists in the violent appropriation of the real by force. Second, the logic of conversion puts the burden of responsibility on the decision of the subject, who is understood as the centre of decision-making. However, the centrality of the subject has been undermined in late modernity, the epoch of generalized communication, where the subject is deprived of decision-making roles. The subject increasingly plays a multiplicity of social roles that cannot be reduced to a unity, to the Cartesian subject. Indeed, Vattimo observes in Nietzsche the manifestation of the mimetic instinct characteristic of post-modern subjectivity. He writes:

> The image the I has of itself, in short, self-consciousness in its true sense, is now seen as the image of ourselves which others communicate to us (and which we accept and adopt for reasons of security: in order to defend ourselves we must in fact introject others' perceptions of us, making our calculations accordingly; in the struggle for survival, mimicry, camouflage is a crucial instrument).[11]

Vattimo does not speak of conversion, but rather of interpretation as a form of participant knowledge that transforms the interpreter. In fact, to listen to an announcement – rather than corresponding to an ideal order of reason – like that of the death of the moral-metaphysical God, or of the end of metaphysics, 'is an event that transforms the life of the one who receives the announcement – or better, an event that is constituted completely in this transformation'.[12]

Vattimo believes that the link between the kenosis of the gospel and nihilistic philosophy has emerged not just as the clarification of his own biographical experience, but rather

---

[11] Vattimo, 'The Problem of Subjectivity from Nietzsche to Heidegger', *Differentia* (1986), 10.
[12] 'Il Dio che è morto', unpublished paper, forthcoming.

as a collective event. The pervasive return of religion in
contemporary culture increasingly calls for an interpretation
of the present that is no longer grounded in the Enlightenment prejudice against religion, and consequently in the
theories of secularization which maintained that religion
would be wiped out by the modern process of rationalization. Vattimo does not see any contradiction between discourse on the return of God in contemporary culture, and
the story of secularization told, for example, by Max Weber.
In brief, Vattimo argues that the story of a putative secularization paradoxically removes the prejudice of secularism
against the religious message. In other words, modernity is
essential to the recovery of religion. By religion, Vattimo
does not mean belief in a clearly defined body of doctrines;
it is the belief that the nihilistic philosopher may well belong
to the circle of faith. Indeed, what ultimately resists the
demythicizing force of secularization is the doctrine of
charity, understood as love for neighbour and for a community of interpreters, and its symbol is the incarnation of
the Son of God.

Vattimo construes incarnation in terms of kenosis, the
self-emptying and self-abasing of God in Jesus Christ. Yet
the appeal to kenosis has to do less with a clearly recognizable christological doctrine than with an understanding of
secularization, as elimination of the violence of the transcendent principle, the ground that silences all questioning.
Vattimo follows René Girard's hypothesis that Christ's death
and resurrection eliminates the violence of all sacrificial
religion through its very unmasking. 'Christ shows that the
sacred is violence, and opens the way to a new human
history that can be called "secularized".'[13] Moreover, the
sacred is identical with the transcendence of natural religion.
Christ's incarnation, according to Vattimo, reveals that

---

[13] Vattimo, 'Myth and the Fate of Secularization', *Res* (Spring 1985), 35.

Being is not a principle (structure, ground) that can be described or represented to sensible intuition, but rather an event that *occurs* as an announcement of language and is oriented toward spiritualization and kenosis. Kenosis, in turn, is not viewed as the truly objective structure of reality. If this were the case, kenosis - this act of charitable self-exhaustion – would be just another mask of the metaphysical principle that silences questioning through its force and authority. By contrast, Vattimo argues that kenosis shows that the divine is fully involved with historicity, with the horizon of language, insofar as it reveals God as peaceful, dialogical *Word*.

As John Milbank has recently argued, the event of incarnation is 'the protocol which decrees that . . . Christ himself embodies an inexhaustible range of meanings which anticipates every individual and collective future. In fact it is only this coding that unleashes symbolic polysemy . . .'[14] Furthermore, the doctrine of kenosis has historically been linked to that of creation. As Moltmann has suggested, the self-humiliation of God that takes place in creation is fulfilled in the incarnation of the Son. 'God permits an existence different from his own by limiting himself. He withdraws his omnipotence in order to set his image, men and women, free. He allows his world to exist in his eternity.'[15] Milbank has recently shown that the doctrine of kenosis was consistently developed by Hamann as an incarnation of God into language. Thus the emphasis on the self-exhaustion of God into the entire text of nature, the writing of creation. 'By his kenotic act of writing, [God] creates the world and human history as a present sign whose concealment-revealment of the absent God is the possibility of man's free

[14] Milbank, 'The Linguistic Turn as a Theological Turn', in *The Word Made Strange: Theology Language, and Culture* (Oxford: Blackwell Publisher, 1997).
[15] Jürgen Moltmann, *Trinity and the Kingdom of God: The Doctrine of God* (London: SCM Press, 1981), 118.

creative response which unravels gradually through time.'[16]
The point is that the text of creation, as well as that of the
Scriptures, opens the way to an unlimited semiosis. In
Vattimo's language, the text is open to the infinitely repeat-
able movement of interpretation.[17]

Hermeneutic philosophy, then, construes itself as a gene-
alogical interpretation of the transmission of knowledge by
weakening its claims to ultimacy. In this process, a spiritualization of Being takes place. If nihilism is understood as
kenosis, as the self-exhaustion of transcendence, it is devoid
of any apocalyptic features, but announces itself with the
logic of religion. Vattimo explains:

> But the kenosis that occurs as the incarnation of God and
> most recently as secularization and the weakening of Being
> and its strong structures (to the point of dissolution of the
> ideal of truth as objectivity) takes place in accordance with a
> 'law' of religion, at least in the sense that it is not by its own
> decision that the subject is committed to a process of ruin,
> for one finds oneself called to such a commitment by the
> 'thing itself'.[18]

The logic of nihilism coincides with the 'law of kenosis',
the law which carries to its logical conclusion a conception
of historicity as belonging. This history of belonging is
expressed in the notion of the hermeneutic circle proposed
by Dilthey, and later by Heidegger.[19] The circularity derives

[16] Milbank, 'Pleonasm, Speech and Writing', in *The Word Made Strange*, 78.

[17] On Hamann, see also Gwen Griffith Dickinson, *Johan Georg Hamann's Relational
Metacriticism* (Berlin and New York: Walter de Gruyter, 1995), 104

[18] Vattimo, *Beyond Interpretation: The meaning of Hermeneutics for Philosophy*, trans. David
Webb (Cambridge: Polity Press, 1996).

[19] Dilthey's thesis is that the object of understanding (text, culture, myths) in the
human sciences cannot be distinguished from the subject of understanding. The
human subject always already belongs to the matter (text, culture, myth) which he or
she wants to understand; therefore, the object does not 'lie' in front of the interpreter.
On this, see Wilhelm Dilthey, *Introduction to the Human Sciences*, trans. Ramos J.
Betanzos (Detroit: Wayne State University Press, 1988).

from the idea that the object of inquiry does not lie in front of the interpreter, as an object over against a subject. Instead, 'the idea underpinning hermeneutics of the belonging of the interpreter to the "thing" to be interpreted, or more generally to the game of interpretation, mirrors, expresses, repeats and interprets this experience of transcendence.'[20]

The nature of hermeneutic experience is clarified by the kenosis of language to the extent that interpretation is based on the common horizon between the interpreter and the 'thing' itself. Theologically one might say that God does not maintain a neutral position within Being, but rather takes a 'position', which in modern philosophy coincides with that of the subject.[21] By weakening the logos, the incarnation eliminates the idea that there is an underlying substance, a *subjectum*, a will, behind the game of interpretation. The incarnation brings about the dispersion and dissemination of the metaphysical principle constitutive of the subject – that is, the subject as the centre of interpretation – through an act which the subject has not chosen. The trace of the divine lies precisely in the initiative coming from the outside, to which the subject responds through an act of interpretation. Vattimo can speak of God as the one who is incarnated into language or, better, into an announcement which has lost the oppressive weight of the foundational principle. God is disclosed as a trace that makes itself felt in our language, and

---

[20] Vattimo, *Beyond Interpretation*, 53.

[21] Bakhtin offers a similar view of the incarnation. He writes:

> No one can assume a position toward the I and the other that is neutral. The abstract cognitive standpoint lacks any axiological approach, since the axiological attitude requires that one should occupy a unique place in the unitary event of Being – that one should be embodied. Any valuation is an act of assuming an individual position in being; even God had to incarnate himself in order to bestow mercy, to suffer and to *forgive* – had to descend, as it were, from the abstract standpoint of justice. (M. M. Bakhtin, 'Author and Hero in Aesthetic Activity', in *Art and Answerability*, ed. and trans. Michal Holquist and Vladimir Liapunov; Austin: University of Texas Press, 1990, 129).

which appeals to us through the dialogical force of charity. In turn, if charity is understood in the light of kenosis, the self-exhaustion of God, then it constitutes the most sublime act of abandonment for the sake of the other. To participate in the hermeneutic experience, then, might mean to welcome the other in the name of the dialogical principle of charity, that is, by listening to the non-violent reasons of the other.

Contemporary philosophy no longer conceives of the subject in terms of dialectical synthesis and unity, but rather in terms of rupture and interpretative hubris. 'Being, even after the end of metaphysics, remains modeled on the subject; but the split subject, which is the overman, can no longer correspond to Being, thought of in terms of fullness, force, determination, eternity, deployed actuality, as the tradition always recognized it.'[22] Contemporary culture identifies the postmodern subject with the hubris and conflict of interpretation. For Vattimo, then, conflicting interpretations trigger a charitable recognition of belonging to a common history.

By elaborating the experience of the postmodern subject, Vattimo takes over the charitable (peaceful) strategy announced in the kenosis of the logos by carrying secularization to its conclusion. Incarnation is an archetypical occurrence of secularization.[23] But is the history of salvation, which ensues from the Christian announcement of incarnation, related to the history of interpretation? Vattimo writes:

> Even if interpretation continues after the resurrection of
> Jesus (indeed by virtue of the resurrection, as its continuation
> and authentication), this means that interpretation and sal-
> vation, too, have a history which is not only an accidental

[22] Vattimo, *Al di là del soggetto*, 36.
[23] Vattimo, 'Storia della salvezza, storia dell'interpretazione', Micromega 3 (1992), 109.

occurrence crossing above or near their supposedly stable kernels. Rather, this history affects them deeply, in a sense that can only be expressed by emphasizing the 'objective' genitive in the two expressions. Salvation takes shape, takes place, gives itself, and constitutes itself through its history, and thus the history of interpretation, too – through a series of connections that can only with difficulty be frozen into a scheme . . . This history has a meaning and a direction, and the interpretation of Scripture that takes place in it is its constitutive dimension. It is not only a tale of errors, or conversely of close or literal understanding of meaning given once and for all in Scripture (which would be as inessential in themselves as errors). The history of salvation continues as history of interpretation in the strong sense in which Jesus himself was the living, incarnate interpretation of Scripture.[24]

This passage implies that the self-exhaustion of Being as announcement, as the occurrence of interpretation, has not stopped the history of interpretation. The narration of incarnation does not reveal once and for all the ground and principle of reality, the true description of reality. Nor does it reveal the essence of the future as the Eternal, as if it were the true description of the life to come. On the contrary, it sets in motion a history in which Being grows, increases together with the constant movement of interpretation. Being grows into the interpretations that follow one another because it manifests itself as the very *history* of interpretation. This means, for Vattimo, that by virtue of the history of interpretation *Being enters fully into time*. This is what he means when he says that Being is time-language, the transmission of messages in the historical-natural language that we inherit from the past.

In his *Lectures on the Philosophy of Religion*, Hegel speaks similarly of the spiritual interpretation of the Christic event

[24] Ibid., 112

as the turning-point in the history of Spirit. 'The history of
resurrection and ascension of Christ to the right hand of
God begins at the point where this history receives a spiritual
interpretation.'[25] The turning-point in the history of salvation is thus its interpretation of God's appearance into
history. Hegel's conclusions, however, seem to go in the
opposite direction of weak thought. The self-lowering of
God in the event of incarnation represents only a transitional
moment within the triumphant procession of Spirit towards
absolute knowledge. By contrast, for Vattimo the incarnation reveals the intimate vocation of the divine towards
spiritualization, dilution and weakening. Kenosis is not the
stage of humiliation in the triumphant life of the divine, the
temporary absorption of the divine into the negative structures of finitude, but rather the very essence of the divine.
Does Vattimo mean to say, then, that the vocation of the
divine being is to vanish?

If kenosis is interpreted as the realization of the vanishing
God, it clashes against the paradoxical structures that have
often been noticed in the discourses on the death of God.
Either God *was* not in the first place, or the vanishing God
concerns the death of the moral-metaphysical God. Vattimo
observes that Nietzsche's announcement of the death of God
may well be interpreted as the death of the moral-metaphysical God. This death, however, does not settle the question
concerning the divine being. Indeed, Nietzsche himself left
open the possibility that new gods might be created; in other
words, he did not close off the possibility of a renewal of
religious experience. Rather, Nietzsche's nihilism opens,
paradoxically, the way to the recovery of the divine in our
culture. The disappearance of the moral-metaphysical God
(the foundation principle of metaphysics), then, may signify

[25] Hegel, *Lectures on the Philosophy of Religion*, ed. Peter Hodgson (Berkeley: University
of California Press, 1988).

that the divine source may announce itself in the drift of interpretation. A privileged access to the divine source, whether in the present or in the future, no longer seems possible. The sole source of which one can become aware seems to be given in the weakened form of interpretation, message, sending.

In the final analysis, what is at stake in Vattimo's argument – about the analogy between the kenosis of language and the announcement of nihilistic philosophy – is the hope that the literal sense of the truths of religion, the experience of faith may be opened to the explicit recognition of the heterogeneous dimensions of existence. From the perspective of kenosis, then, existence appears as infinite plurality. For Vattimo, it is precisely when we dare to look at the West as the land of the twilight of metaphysics that we may find in full our humanity, with its divine aspirations, It is a humanity that glimpses the trace of a God who *occurs* as weak announcement, a God that emerges from infinite dialogues and interpretations.

Belief

Return

For a long time I woke up early to go to mass, before school, before the office, before university lectures. This book could begin thus, perhaps even punning that it concerns 'la recherche du *temple* perdu'. But what if I were to take the liberty not just to pun but to write in the first person? I am aware that I have never written in this way except in debates, polemics or letters to the editor. Never in essays or texts of a professional character, whether critical or philosophical. Here the question arises because the following pages take up themes from a long double interview, together with Sergio Quinzio, conducted in 1995 for *La Stampa* by Claudio Altarocca, and there we spoke in the first person; but also because the theme of religion and faith seems to require a necessarily 'personal' and 'engaged writing', even though it will neither be primarily narrative nor clearly refer back to a narrating-believing I.[1]

Furthermore: it seems necessary to clarify from the outset that I have resolved to speak and write on faith and religion, because I take the subject matter to be more than a concern of my own renewed personal interest in this theme; the decisive factor is that I sense a renewed interest in religion in the cultural atmosphere around me. It is certainly a vague reason, itself very subjective, little more than an impression. However, by seeking to justify and document it I hope to

[1] Sergio Quinzio (1927–96) was a religious writer, theologian, and essayist. Among his works see: *Commento alla bibbia*, 4 vols (Milan: Adelphi, 1972–6); *La fede sepolta* (Milan: Adelphi, 1978); *La croce e il nulla* (Milan: Adelphi, 1984).

make some progress towards the clarification of this theme. The renewed religious sensibility I 'feel' around me, which appears to be imprecise and not definable with any rigour, corresponds well to the topic (to believe in belief) around which my argument revolves.

Hence, a mixture of individual and collective (individually held!) facts. It is true that I have reached a point in life when it seems obvious, predictable, even a bit banal to come back to the question of faith. To restate it: at least for me, the matter is precisely the return of a thematic (a word that tells us little, though we shall use it here) that has engaged me in the past. Is it possible, to speak parenthetically, for the question of faith not to be a restatement? It is a good question, because, as I shall show in the following pages, the religious problem seems to be always the recovery of an experience that one has somehow already had. None of us in our western culture – and perhaps not in any culture – begins from zero with the question of religious faith.

The relation to the sacred, God, the ultimate reasons for existence that are in general what religion is about (let me say once and for all that I shall use these terms without seeking rigorous definitions, at least in this sort of public conversation), is lived by all of us as the re-presentation of the core contents of consciousness we had forgotten, put aside, buried in a not quite unconscious realm of our mind, that we may even at times have violently dismissed as an ensemble of childish ideas belonging to other epochs of or lives, perhaps even errors into which we had fallen, from which we should free ourselves.

I emphasize this matter of 'recovery', because it concerns one of the themes of the argument I shall develop here, which seeks to characterize 'secularization' as the constitutive trait of an authentic religious experience. Now, secularization means precisely a relation of provenance from a sacred core from which one has moved away, but which nevertheless remains active even in its 'fallen', distorted version, reduced to pure worldly terms. Believers may obviously read the idea of recovery and return as a sign of the search for the origin, namely, the creature's dependence on God. Yet I believe that it is just as significant and important not to forget that this recovery is also the recognition of a necessarily fallen relation. As in the forgetting of Being of which Heidegger spoke, here too (analogy, allegory; once again, are we speaking of secularization of the religious message?) it is less a case of recollecting the forgotten origin by making it present again than of recollecting that we have always already forgotten it, and that the recollection of this forgetfulness and this distance constitutes the sole authentic religious experience.

Then how does religion 'return' – if indeed, as it seems to me, it does return – in my–our contemporary experience? As far as I am personally concerned, I am not ashamed to say that it is related to the experience of death – of people dear to me, with whom I had planned to share a longer stretch of the journey, in some cases of persons I had always imagined would be around me when my time to pass away came, and indeed that I fancied to be lovable precisely because of their virtue (ironic affection for the world, acceptance of every living being in its limit) in rendering death itself livable and acceptable (as in a line from Hölderlin: 'heilend, begeisternd wie du').[2]

It may be that even beyond these contingent events, what brings back the question of religion at a certain time of life has to do with the physiology of maturity and of getting old. The idea that the 'outside' must coincide with the inside, German idealism's dream (such was the artwork for Hegel, and the work of reason for Fichte), namely that existence will coincide *de facto* with its meaning, is put in

[2] From the poem 'Götterwandelten einst'.

perspective over the course of a lifetime. As a consequence, increasing importance is given to the hope that the coincidence, which seems to be unrealizable within historical time and in the arc of an average human life, may realize itself in a different time-frame. The Kantian postulates of the immortality of the soul and of the existence of God are justified precisely by this type of argument. If the effort to do good, to act in conformity with the moral law, is to make any sense, it must be possible to hope reasonably for goodness (namely, the unity of happiness and virtue) to be realized in another world, since it is clearly not given in this one.

I am not entirely convinced that to forgo belief in the coincidence of existence and meaning in this world is physiological. I am inclined to believe (as in the case of the return of religion, which seems to be a 'collective' fact, in addition to its links with my specific life-experience) that the abandonment of the idealistic dream (in the current and in the technico-philosophical sense of the term) is above all linked to specific historical circumstances: for someone whose life coincided perfectly with a long revolutionary process of renewal and enthusiastic construction of the world (one recalls what Sartre says about the 'group in fusion' in the *Critique of Dialectical Reason*)[3] the renunciation might not be as inevitable. Yet, if such a possibility seems absurd in the case of the revolution (and this is what happens in Sartre when the moments of plenitude to be fused – fatally? – fall back on the practico-inert, on routine, on bureaucratization), it may be less unthinkable, for example, in the case of an artist's life.

No matter how one resolves this (not at all banal) problem, I cannot take the experience of a permanent discrep-

---

[3] Jean-Paul Sartre, *Critique of Dialectical Reason*, trans. Quinton Hoare (London: Verso, 1991).

ancy between existence and meaning to be an exclusively physiological fact; rather, it appears as the decisive consequence of a historical process in which projects, dreams of renewal, hopes even for (political) redemption, to which I had been deeply committed were shattered in a wholly contingent way. Perhaps Pascal, the theoriest of *divertissement*, might say that even if one were to succeed in living one's whole life in a state of uninterrupted projectural intensity, one would still only be concealing the impending possibility of individual death, from which there is in view no reasonable hope of deliverance. There is, perhaps, no theoretical solution to this problem. It may be that the Christian hope in the resurrection of the flesh invites us not to resolve it too 'easily' by resigning oneself.to defer any possible fulfilment in the beyond. Whether it concerns the flesh or its resurrection, it seems to say that the substance of Christian hope comprises the idea that the fulfilment of redemption is not wholly discontinuous with our history and with our earthly projects.

It should already have become clear from these last passages that the return of religion and of the problem of faith is not unrelated to world history, and is not merely reducible to a transition between life-stages always conceived according to the same pattern (whenever people get old, they all begin to think more about the beyond, therefore about God). Yet even the historical circumstances bringing back the problem of faith share a trait in common with the physiology of ageing: in both cases the problem of God is posed in relation to the encounter with a limit as the occurrence of a defeat: we believed that we could realize justice on earth, but now reckon that it is no longer possible and turn our hopes to God. Death hovers over us as an ineluctable event, we escape from despair by turning to God and his promise to welcome us into his eternal kingdom. Shall God be discovered only where one clashes against something utterly unpleasant? As in the way the expression, 'God's will be done' is used only when something goes badly wrong, and not, for example, when one wins the lottery?

The very return of religion in our culture seems to be bound up with the apparent insolubility, with the instruments of reason and technology, of a number of pressing problems confronting late-modern humanity: issues above all in bioethics, from genetic manipulation to ecology, and problems concerning the explosion of violence in the new conditions of existence within mass society. A number of good objections may be raised against the idea that God is to be recognized where one comes up against unsurpassable limits – conflicts, defeats and negativity – even from the believers' perspective (I am thinking of Dietrich Bonhoeffer's polemic against the idea of God as a stop-gap), but above all from the perspective of 'lay' reason.[4] If there is a God, he is surely not responsible only for our troubles, nor is he someone who can be known mainly through our failures. Yet this way of experiencing God is bound up with a certain conception of transcendence, to which I shall return in the course of my argument.

It is as if the prejudice of our culture and the mental habits inherited from an atavistic kind of 'natural' religion – one that sees God in the threatening powers of nature, in earthquakes and thunder that frighten us at a primitive stage of civilization and from which we could only defend ourselves with beliefs, magical practices and superstuitions – led us to conceive transcendence as the opposite of every rationality, as a power disclosing its alterity only by negating everything that appears to be reasonable and good. It is quite possible that within the horizon of such prejudices divine

[4] Letter of 29 May 1944, in *Letters and Papers from Prison* (New York: Macmillan, 1972).

transcendence reveals itself primarily in this guise. Yet the experience of faith could well lead towards the consummation and dissolution of this initial manifestation – following the evangelical saying 'I no longer call you servants, but friends' – while a certain theology and experience of religion, even the Catholic Church's authoritarianism, appear determined to establish it as definitive and true.

That God's return in our culture and in the contemporary mindset might have something to do with the sense of defeat with which Reason faces many problems that have deepened in recent years, does not mean that the threatening and negative image of divine transcendence needs to be treated as insuperable, insofar as these traits effectively secure alterity with regard to the simply 'human'. However, the dramatic nature of these unresolved problems is only one of the factors that today determine the renewed actuality of religion. One may recall at least two other kinds of reason, one specifically 'political', the other philosophical. The political reasons may be traced back to the decisive role played by Pope Wojtyla in the erosion and dissolution of the east European communist regimes. Outside Christian and Catholic Europe, the political presence of the Pope is paralleled by the increasing political importance of Islamic religious hierarchies (with all their differences) in the Muslim world.

One might say that the new political significance of religious hierarchies is not a cause but an effect of the renewed sensibility to religion. Although it is difficult to settle the issue once and for all, it seems more likely to me that here politics is a cause, not least because it explains the situation better and more directly. According to the other hypothesis, one would have to appeal simply to Providence, which today mysteriously draws human beings closer to God, or to the always too general discourses on the gravity of the contemporary crisis, which – according to the mechanism referred to before – should explain why God has again become such a central point of reference for our culture. To be sure, even the political significance of religious hierarchies is not born out of nothing. For example: the attention reserved for the ayatollahs of various persuasions, not only by many Muslims in their own countries but also by western governments and public opinion, would not have been possible without the petrol 'war' in the seventies and the terrorism of Islamic fundamentalism in the following decades, which had more to do with the epoch of the end of colonialism than with religious renewal.

A similar argument can be put forward for the Christian world and Wojtyla's papacy. His engagement as a Polish citizen against the regimes of the Soviet bloc took place when those regimes were beginning to break up for reasons that were not primarily religious. Their fall finally enhanced the significance of the Pope's action and contributed to granting him a new authority in the eyes of public opinion. As far as Italy itself is concerned another event that has recently burst into view, and which is not exclusively linked to the Polish Pope's reign, seems to have been decisive: the end of political Catholicism that had, in Italy, signified a strict link between choice of faith and electoral orientation (and obligation). The erosion of this link between faith and politics – which has finally made it possible for people who are not Christian Democrats to hear the Church's teaching and has caught the anticlerical tradition in Italian lay culture itself unprepared – was not primarily the consequence of religious maturity, but the effect of a different configuration in the political landscape: the weakening of communism, the fall of the two blocs, the end of the struggle between the Good Empire and the 'Evil Empire' (as Reagan once called the USSR).

These are some possible 'external' and socio-political explanations for the renewal of religion – as a renewed interest in the question of faith and as a readiness to listen to the teaching of the churches, in Italy, of the Catholic Church.

Return and philosophy

Alongside the explanations mentioned above, another set of transformations in the theoretical world of thought has been determinant in the renewal of religion. Whereas for many decades in this century religions appeared, according to the Enlightenment and positivistic idea, as 'residual' forms of experience increasingly destined to be deleted by the imposition of the 'modern' form of life (technico-scientific rationalization of social life, political democracy, and so on), today they appear again as possible guides for the future.

The 'end of modernity', or in any case its crisis, has also been accompanied by the dissolution of the main philosophical theories that claimed to have done away with religion: positivist scientism, Hegelian and then Marxist historicism. Today there are no longer strong, plausible philosophical reasons to be atheist, or at any rate to dismiss religion. Atheistic rationalism had taken two forms in modernity: belief in the exclusive truth of the experimental natural sciences, and faith in history's progress towards the full emancipation of humanity from any transcendent authority.

These two types of rationalism were often mixed together, for example, in the positivistic conception of progress. In each of these perspectives, there was only a provisional place for religion, which was regarded as an error destined to be dismissed by scientific rationality, or a moment to be overcome by reason's unfolding towards fuller and 'truer' forms of self-consciousness. Today, however, both belief in objective truth and faith in the progress of Reason towards full transparency appear to have been defeated. We are all by now used to the fact that disenchantment has also produced a radical disenchantment with the idea of disenchantment itself; or, in other words, that demythification has finally turned against itself, recognizing that even the ideal of the elimination of myth is a myth. To be sure, this outcome of modern thought is not peaceably recognized by all; but the untenability of scientistic and historicist rationalism – both of which repudiated the very possibility of religion – has been widely accepted as a given in our culture.

My argument has its point of departure here in Nietzsche's and Heidegger's notions of nihilism as the end-point of modernity, and in the consequent task of thinking understood as the recognition of the end of metaphysics. Since the way I advance my interpretation of the return of religion is deeply informed by these notions, I shall give at least a brief description of them here. The Nietzschean notions of nihilism and 'will to power' announce an interpretation of modernity as the final consummation of the belief that Being and reality are 'objective' data which thinking ought to contemplate in order to bring itself into conformity with their laws. In a famous chapter from *The Twilight of the Idols*,[5] under the heading 'How the Real World at Last Became a Fable',[6] Nietzsche retraces the stages of this consummation. At first Greek philosophy conceived the truth of the world in a metaphysical beyond – Plato's stable and definitive world of ideas was supposed to guarantee the possibility of rigorous knowledge of the mobile and mutable things of everyday experience. Then, much later in the same philo-

---

[5] Nietzsche, *Twilight of the Idols*, trans. R. J. Hollingdale (Harmondsworth: Penguin, 1968).
[6] The published translation is 'How the World at Last Became a Myth' Following the Italian translation, Vattimo uses the word 'fable', instead of 'myth'.

sophical history of the idea of truth, emerged the Kantian discovery that the world of experience is co-constituted by the human subject's intervention (without the a priori forms of sensibility and the intellect there is no 'world', but only the 'thing-in-itself' of which we know nothing except that we cannot deny its existence). Finally thinking becomes aware that what is actually real is, as the positivists assert, a 'positive' fact, a given established by science. Establishing, however, is precisely the act of the human subject (though not of the individual subject), and the reality of the world of which we speak is identified as the 'product' of scientific experiments and technological apparatus. There is no longer a 'true world' or, better, truth is reduced entirely to what is 'posited' by the human being, namely 'will to power'.

Heidegger basically takes over this Nietzschean reconstruction of the history of western culture, though, for him, this means that nihilism (the recognition that Being and reality are merely the subject's position, product) heralds the end of metaphysics, namely the thought (this is the meaning of the term in Heidegger) that identifies Being with the objectively given, the thing before me, before which I can only contemplate in silent admiration. This identification is, for Heidegger, unacceptable; not because it might be revealed as an error, which would have to be replaced by a truer, but always 'objective', vision of what Being really is – in this way we would still be wholly within the metaphysics of objectivity. According to Heidegger, the reasons for dismissing metaphysics are those shared by much of the philosophical and literary avant-garde thinking of the early twentieth century (I am thinking of Ernst Bloch's *Spirit of Utopia*, published in 1918, which is a sort of *summa* of the avant-garde's expressionist mentality): the metaphysics of objectivity culminates in a thinking that identifies the truth of Being with the calculable, measurable and definitively manipulable object of techno-science. Now, this conception of Being as measurable and manipulable object conceals the basis of the world that Adorno called 'the world of total organization', where even the human subject will fatally tend to become raw material, a part of the general mechanism of production and consumption.

Heidegger's development of a philosophy that strives to think Being in non-metaphysical terms takes its point of departure from his critique of metaphysics, which, I repeat, does not have principally a theoretical but an ethical and political basis (the point is not to counterpose to the vision of Being as objectivity a more adequate, truer conception, which would still be objective, but rather to quit a horizon of thought that is an enemy of freedom and of the historicity of existing). With regard to the developments in philosophy of the early twentieth-century spirit of the avant-garde (Lukác's critical Marxism, the critical theory of the Frankfurt school, the various existentialist trends, and so on), Heidegger seems to hold the most radical and consistent position – obviously, I cannot say it is the 'truer' position, at least not in the sense of an adequate description of an object, Being, given before us.

Heidegger's thought seems both radical and consistent with regard to my experience of the human condition in late modernity, an experience whose nihilistic traits seem plain enough: as science speaks increasingly little of objects that can be compared with those in everyday experience, it is no longer clear what to call 'reality' – what I see and feel or what is described in books about physics or astrophysics? Technology and the production of commodities increasingly configure the world as an artificial world, where one cannot distinguish between natural, basic needs and those induced and manipulated by advertisement, so that here too there is no longer a measuring-stick to distinguish the real from the 'invented'. History too, after the end of colonialism and the dissolution of Eurocentric prejudice, has lost its unitary meaning and broken up into many histories that are irreducible to a single guiding thread.

The nihilism in which Nietzsche and Heidegger see the outcome and, I believe, the meaning of western history (after all Heidegger insists on the etymology of the word 'Occident': the land of the twilight, of the sunset of being), does not seem, from their perspective, an errancy of the human spirit that one might quit by changing course, namely, by discovering that Being is actually not only will to power, but something else. A correction of this kind, in Heidegger's view, would not avoid the trap of objectivistic metaphysics. Who, and with what tools, could establish by experiment that Being is not the 'product', position, object of the will to power – since she or he would have to establish such a truth via a procedure that is scientifically trustworthy, with methods, tools and calculations? From Heidegger's perspective, the efforts to discover Being in lived immediacy, not yet entrapped in the schemes of the scientific method so as to avoid the mechanism of objectivation, are empty as well.

To be sure, these alternatives to Nietzschean-Heideggerian nihilism deserve attention and should be discussed in greater analytical depth (I have tried to do so elsewhere). On this occasion I shall merely observe that my reflection on the return of religion has its point of departure in the idea that Heidegger and Nietzsche are right; and that above and beyond the theoretical reasons that seem persuasive, my preference for the Heideggerian 'solution' to contemporary philosophical problems is conditioned, and profoundly inspired by the Christian inheritance.

Christian inheritance and nihilism

I am speaking of inheritance not only because in my personal experience adherence to the Christian message is something from the past that has become present again via reflections on the events and theoretical transformations I have spoken of. Rather, I believe that one ought to speak of Christian inheritance in a much broader sense that would concern our culture in general, which has also become what it is because it has been 'worked' and forged in friendship by the Christian message, or more generally by the biblical revelation (Old and New Testament).

Let me try to clarify and simplify this point. I am aware that I have a preference for Nietzsche and Heidegger in part (or perhaps above all) because, over against other philosophical projects that I have come across, their thesis, based on a given interpretation of their work, seems to be above all in harmony with a specifically Christian religious substratum that has remained a living part of me. Moreover, that it has become present again is due at least in part to the fact that, having distanced myself from the Christian inheritance (or so I believed), it was above all with the writings of Nietzsche and Heidegger that I spent my time and in their light that I lived and interpreted my existential condition in late-modern society. In short: I have begun to take Christianity seriously again because I have constructed a philosophy inspired by Nietzsche and Heidegger, and have interpreted my experience in the contemporary world in the light of it; yet in all probability I constructed my philosophy with a preference for these authors precisely because I started with the Christian inheritance, which I have now found again, though, in reality, I had never abandoned it.

I would not insist so much on analysing the 'circularity' of my situation (is it not scandalous, from a logical perspective?) were it not for my belief, based on precisely these ideas (but just on these ideas? Another circle), that the circularity also characterizes the relation of the late-modern world to the Judaeo-Christian inheritance.

Let us go carefully. First of all, what kind of relation can there be between my personal Christian inheritance – the fact that I grew up as a practising, even fervent, Catholic committed to living up to the teachings of Jesus Christ – and Nietzschean-Heideggerian nihilism?

It is not by chance that these reflections finally found the courage to take shape into a text on the occasion of a conversation with Sergio Quinzio. Quinzio was one of the authors (with René Girard, to whom I shall return) who most influenced my nihilistic rediscovery of Christianity, even though his understanding of the nexus between Christianity and nihilism ultimately differs from mine. I should say that the Christian inspiration makes itself felt in my reading of Heidegger precisely in its characterization as 'weak'. 'Weak thought' is an expression I used in an essay from the early eighties that became the introductory text to a volume of essays I edited with Pier Aldo Rovatti, and which ended up as the label of a philosophical trend, or (even) a school of thought, whose borders are even now uncertain, and which was in no way united around a common core of identifiable theses.[7] For me, the primary meaning of this expression – which I coined by drawing from an essay by Carlo Augusto Viano, who became one of the harshest and most unfriendly critics of weak thought[8] –

---

[7] See 'Dialettica, differenza, pensiero debole', in *Il pensiero debole*, ed. P. A. Rovatti and Gianni Vattimo, 12th edn (Milan: Feltrinelli, 1998); 'Dialectic, Difference, Weak Thought', trans. Thomas Harrison, New School of Social Research, *Graduate Faculty Philosophy Journal* 10 (1984).

[8] On Viano, see the essay on 'La ragione, l'abbondanza e la credenza', in the volume

is not the idea of a thinking that is more aware of its own limits, that abandons its claims to global and metaphysical visions, but above all a theory of weakening as the constitutive character of Being in the epoch of the end of metaphysics. If, indeed, Heidegger's critique of objectivistic metaphysics cannot be carried forward by replacing the latter with a more adequate conception of Being (still thought of as an object), one will have to think Being as not identified, in any sense, with the presence characteristic of the object. But this, as I believe is easily shown, also entails that the history of nihilism cannot be treated merely as a history of errors: as if metaphysics – which identifies Being with the object and ultimately reduces it to a product of the will to power – were something that concerned merely the ideas of human beings, and specifically the ideas of western philosophers and scientists, whereas Being lay beyond all this in objective independence. In short (for a more detailed and hopefully more convincing discussion, I have to refer the reader to other writings of mine), if one wants to think Being in non-metaphysical terms one ought to conceive of metaphysics as the history of Being, and not as a history of human errors. But this means that Being has a nihilistic vocation and that diminishment, withdrawal and weakening are the traits that Being assigns to itself in the epoch of the end of metaphysics and of the becoming problematic of objectivity.

Here hopefully one will begin to see more clearly why my interpretation of Heidegger's thought as 'weak ontology' or weakening can be thought of as the rediscovery of Christianity and as the outcome of its permanent action. I do not know exactly when in my itinerary I made this substantial link, certainly not on the occasion of my first

---

edited by A. G. Gargani, *Crisi della ragione* (Turin: Einaudi, 1979); and the pamphlet against weak thought, *Va, pensiero* (Turin: Einaudi, 1985).

formulation of the 'weak' interpretation of Heidegger in 1979. It is possible that it happened in the wake of the experiences of suffering, sickness and death of people who were dear to me a few years later; but it is more likely that I made this link by reflecting on René Girard's work, which I approached by reading *Of Things Hidden since the Foundation of the World*, (translated by P. Gregory; London: Athlone Press, 1987) in the Italian translation published by Adelphi in 1983, which I reviewed for a journal. The fact of the matter is that at a certain moment I found myself thinking that the weak reading of Heidegger and the idea that the history of Being has as a guiding thread the weakening of strong structures, of the claimed peremptoriness of the real that is given 'there, outside', like a wall against which one beats one's head, and that in this way makes itself known as effectively real (it is an image of the reality of Being and ultimately of God's transcendence that I heard from Umberto Eco, during a debate in 1994), was nothing but the transcription of the Christian doctrine of the incarnation of the Son of God.

I know well that the term 'transcription', which I use here for lack of a better word, conceals a number of problems. Above all: is transcription the truth of the original text, or just a faded copy that would benefit from the reconstruction of its authentic redaction? In the following pages, the meaning of this relation between philosophy (weak thought) and the Christian message that I am able to think of only in terms of secularization, that is, weakening, incarnation, will hopefully become less obscure.

Yet does it make sense to conceive of the Christian doctrine concerning the incarnation of the Son of God as an announcement of an ontology of weakening? Here my reading (which is not necessarily faithful to the letter of the text, though I have reasons to believe that the author would not object to the main thesis) of René Girard's work comes into play. Before *Of Things Hidden since the Foundation of the World*, Girard had published *Violence and the Sacred* (translated by P. Gregory; London: Athlone Press, 1988), a text on philosophical anthropology, as we may call it, just to underline that it is not a work of cultural anthropology in the usual sense but a theory on the origins and developments of human civilization, grounded on the thesis that from the purely natural, human perspective, what is called sacred is deeply related to violence.

Basically Girard claims that human societies are held together by a powerful drive, the mimetic drive, which is also the source of crises that threaten to destroy them when the need to imitate others erupts into the will to possess things belonging to others and engenders a war of all against all. Then harmony is re-established only by finding the scapegoat on which to focus the violence, rather in the way that the anger of the fans at a soccer stadium tends to discharge itself upon the referee. Since it really works – ending war and re-establishing the basis of society – the scapegoat is invested with sacred attributes and made into a cultic object, while still retaining the status of sacrificial victim. These 'natural' characteristics of the sacred are retained in the Bible: Christian theology perpetuates the victim-based mechanism conceiving Jesus Christ as the 'perfect victim', who, by virtue of the infinite value of his sacrifice (just as the human-divine person of Jesus is infinite) fully satisfies God's need for justice in regard to Adam's sin. Girard argues, with good reason, that this victim-based reading of Scripture is wrong. Jesus' incarnation did not take place to supply the father with a victim adequate to his wrath; rather, Jesus came into the world precisely to reveal and abolish the nexus between violence and the sacred. He was put to death because such a revelation was intolerable to a humanity rooted in the violent tradition of sacrificial religions.

That the Christian churches continue to speak of Jesus as a sacrificial victim testifies to the survival of powerful traces of natural religion in Christianity. Yet the biblical revelation (Old and New Testament) also represents the long process of God's education of humanity, which is proceeding towards an increasingly clear-cut break from the natural religions of sacrifice. This process has yet to be completed: this is the meaning of the survival of the victim-based mechanism in Christian theology.

Incarnation and secularization

Apart from the not always explicit recognition that divine pedagogy is still at work, namely that revelation is not entirely fulfilled, what seems decisive in Girard's theses (which, I repeat, are richer and more articulate than they appear here, and could be interpreted differently) is the idea of the incarnation as the dissolution of the sacred as violence. Here Girard takes up the heritage of much twentieth-century theology, which has insisted on the radical difference between the Christian faith and 'religion', the latter being understood as humanity's natural inclination to think of itself as dependent upon a supreme being – which ends up being only the projection of human desires, precisely because it responds to such a natural inclination, thereby lending itself to the powerful critique inaugurated by Feuerbach and then carried on by Marx.

To move closer to the nihilistic recovery of Christianity, it is sufficient to go just a little bit beyond Girard by acknowledging that the natural sacred is violent not only insofar as the victim-based mechanism presupposes a divinity thirsty for vengeance, but also insofar as it attributes to such a divinity all the predicates of omnipotence, absoluteness, eternity and 'transcendence' with respect to humanity that are precisely the attributes assigned to God by natural theologies, even by those which think of themselves as the prolegomena to the Christian faith. In short, Girard's violent God is from this standpoint the God of metaphysics, what metaphysics called *ipsum esse subsistens*, the summation in pre-eminent form of all the characters of objective being as thought by metaphysics. The dissolution of metaphysics is also the end of this image of God, the death of God of which Nietzsche spoke.

Yet the end of the metaphysical God does not prepare the rediscovery of the Christian God only insofar as it removes the prejudice of natural religion. If the meaning of the end of metaphysics is to reveal in Being an essential inclination to assert its truth through weakening, weak ontology will not be just a negative preparation for the return of religion; this is what happens in philosophies of religion based on existentialism which oppose to natural theology (which claims to demonstrate immediately the existence of God as the cause of the world) a negative anthropology that demonstrates the need for God (the omnipotent and absolute God of metaphysics) by starting with the unresolvable problematic of the human condition. By contrast, the incarnation, that is, God's abasement to the level of humanity, what the New Testament calls God's kenosis, will be interpreted as the sign that the non-violent and non-absolute God of the post-metaphysical epoch has as its distinctive trait the very vocation for weakening of which Heideggerian philosophy speaks.[9]

What do philosophy and Christian religious thought 'draw' from the recognition of this proximity? Since I have resolved to speak in the first person here, I confess that I

[9] Philippians 2:7.

experienced the clarification of this notion of weak ontology as the 'transcription' of the Christian message as a great event, as a kind of decisive discovery. I believe that this is because it allowed me to re-establish a continuity with my own personal religious origin; as if it allowed me to return home – though this did not and does not signify a return to the Catholic Church, to its discipline, at once threatening and reassuring. It was like weaving together threads of discourse that had been left hanging, and that now seemed to find coherence and continuity once more.

But it is/was not only a matter of psychological satisfaction. The discovery of the substantial link between the history of Christian revelation and the history of nihilism means nothing more and nothing less than a confirmation of the validity of Heidegger's discourse on the end of metaphysics. Richard Rorty, a thinker well disposed to Heidegger, recently argued that one of Heidegger's serious limits was to call 'the history of Being' an event which unfolds in no more than a hundred books or so of the western tradition that constitutes the philosophical canon in which Heidegger grew up, and whose limits and contingency Heidegger should have acknowledged, reducing his claims and treating his ontology as the private reconstruction of his family history. However, if the history of the West is interpreted in terms of nihilism, then Heidegger would not be merely the author of an autobiographical novel. And the history of the Christian religion would not be a part of western history, but a guiding thread within it.

My reflections on Girard (as well as on Quinzio's analysis of the history of western civilization as proof of Christianity's 'failure', given that we have witnessed the Holocaust two thousand years after Christ) paved the way for a conception of secularization characteristic to modern western history as an event within Christianity linked positively to Jesus' message and to a conception of the history of modernity as a weakening and dissolution of (metaphysical) Being. I have often told myself, and repeat it to myself over and over, that this 'coming together' of the pieces of my personal religious-philosophical *puzzle* is too good to be true. Yet, the prejudiced distrust towards what appears to be reasonable and persuasive would still be an uncritical way of accepting an apocalyptic (or at least necessarily fragmentary) conception of Being; a kind of negative theology that would be content with the recognition that God cannot be adequately named by any of the names assigned to him. Hence, instead of objecting that this is too good to be true (or, the same, that modernity or the West or secularization are terms which are too generic to have any 'objective' validity), I look forward to anyone who disagrees with me proposing a more persuasive interpretative hypothesis.

The keystone of this argument is the term 'secularization'. This, as is well known, indicates the process of 'drifting' that removed modern lay civilization from its sacral origin. If the natural sacred is the violent mechanism that Jesus came to unveil and undermine, it is possible that secularization – which also constitutes the Church's loss of temporal authority and human reason's increasing autonomy from its dependence upon an absolute God, a fearful Judge who so transcends our ideas about good and evil as to appear as a capricious or bizarre sovereign – is precisely a positive effect of Jesus' teaching, and not a way of moving away from it. It may be that Voltaire himself is a positive effect of the Christianization of mankind, and not a blasphemous enemy of Christ.

However, the point here is not to seek paradoxical and picturesque implications. The 'positive' meaning of secularization, namely the idea that lay modernity is constituted above all as a continuation and desacralizing interpretation of the biblical message, may be seen, for example, in Max Weber's analysis of the sociology of religion, remembered for its thesis that modern capitalism is the effect of the Protestant ethic, and more generally for the idea that the rationalization of modern society is unthinkable outside the Judaeo-Christian monotheistic perspective. One can also speak of modernity as a secularization in other senses, which are themselves still linked to the idea of desacralizing the violent, authoritarian and absolute sacred of natural religion: for example, the transformation of state power, from the divinely sanctioned to constitutional monarchy up to contemporary representative democracies, can also easily (if not exclusively) be described in terms of secularization.

Another author to whom I have often referred in speaking of the secularization of modernity is Norbert Elias, whose work for the most part seeks to illustrate the modern transformations in power as formalizations that increasingly diminish the absoluteness of the 'sacred' person's sovereignty. In the course of this process modern subjectivity is secularized as well. For on entering into a network of power and social relations more complex than those with the sovereign person, the subject has necessarily to articulate itself in terms of a system of mediations that make subjectivity less peremptory and, as it were, predispose it to become the subject matter of psychoanalysis. Indeed, this represents a powerful factor in secularization insofar as it removes the illusion regarding the sacred ultimacy of consciousness (the ego's wound to narcissism, as Freud called it).

It might be remarked that the extension of the notion of secularization to phenomena that are so different borders on the arbitrary. Fair enough. For this reason, it seems more appropriate to speak in more general terms of weakening, with secularization taken as its pre-eminent case. The term 'secularization', however, remains central because it seems to underline the religious sense of all this process. This is what I mean when I say that weak ontology is a transcription of the Christian message. If, as I said, I acknowledge that my preference for a weak reading of Heidegger with respect to other philosophical perspectives follows from my Christian inheritance, even the vision of modernity as the last epoch of metaphysics that derives from that ontology will understand itself to have been decisively shaped by religion. The centrality of the concept of secularization expresses precisely this recognition. Hence I believe that one may reasonably concede that not only the capitalist economy (as shown by Weber), but all the principal traits of western civilization as well are structured by their relation to Judaeo-Christian Scripture, the text upon which this civilization is based. While our civilization no longer explicitly professes itself Christian but rather considers itself by and large a dechristianized, post-Christian, lay civilization, it is nevertheless profoundly shaped by that heritage at its source. This is the reason why I speak of a 'positive' secularization as a characteristic trait of modernity.

Beyond the violence of metaphysics

Establishing the link between secularization as the constitutive trait of modernity and ontology of weakening does not just suggest intriguing developments in the philosophy of history. It also gives weakening and secularization the sense of a critical guiding thread which entails a capacity for making evaluations. This is not because they are 'objective' features of Being to which one must give one's assent or conform, as a metaphysical or historicist-metaphysical position would have it. Moreover, Heidegger's discourse, which, as I have observed all along, is my point of reference, arose precisely out of a reaction against the claims of metaphysical objectivity and its ethico-political implications.

We have sought to think Being outside the metaphysics of objectivity precisely for ethical reasons, and the latter must guide us in our elaboration of the consequences of a non-metaphysical conception of Being, such as an ontology of weakening. To be clear: the Christian inheritance that 'returns' in weak thought is primarily the Christian precept of charity and its rejection of violence. Once again, as always, we find circles: as I shall show in a moment, we derive an ethics of non-violence from weak ontology, yet we are led to weak thought, from its origin in Heidegger's concern with the dangers of the metaphysics of objectivity, by the Christian legacy of the rejection of violence at work within us.

We are able to recognize that the history of Being has a 'reductive', nihilistic meaning, a tendency to assert the truth of Being by reducing the compelling nature of the entities (whether they be the political authority, the threatening and bizarre God of natural religion, or the peremptory finality of the modern subject understood as the guarantor of truth), only because we have been educated by the Christian tradition to think of God not as a master but as a friend, to proclaim that essential things are revealed not to the wise but to the little ones, to believe that whoever does not lose his soul will not save it, and so on. If I say now that, in thinking of the history of Being as guided by the common guiding thread of the reduction of strong structures, I am oriented towards an ethics of non-violence, I am not seeking to legitimize 'objectively' certain maxims of action on the basis of the fact that Being is structured in a certain way; I am merely reformulating, in a different way, the appeal, the call addressing me from the tradition in which I am placed, and of which weak ontology is only a risky interpretation.

If someone (I am thinking of Rorty) were to say to me that there is no need to speak of the history of Being to explain my preference for a world where solidarity and respect for others prevail, rather than war of all against all, I would object that even from the perspective of solidarity and respect it is important to become aware of the roots of our preferences. Indeed, an ethics of respect and solidarity can become reasonable, precise in what it says and capable of holding its own in conversation with others precisely by relating itself explicitly to its provenance.

Since I am not writing a philosophical essay, but telling why and how I have rediscovered religion through my work as a philosophical scholar, I can allow myself to leave some 'gaps' in the argument, that is, problematic points not fully developed. This is the case of the complex circular relationship between the Christian inheritance, weak ontology and an ethics of non-violence. So I shall briefly and provisionally conclude this point: it is true that to 'ground' an ethics of non-violence on an ontology of weakening may seem yet again like a return to metaphysics, for which morality coincided with the recognition of and respect for essences, natural laws and so on. Yet if ontology speaks of Being as something that constitutes itself by withdrawing, whose withdrawal is revealed by the fact that thinking no longer can consider itself the reflection of objective structures but merely a risky interpretation of its heritage (appeals, provenances), then the risk seems to be entirely imaginary, a purely 'logical' phantasm. It is like asserting that even the thesis of weakening is a philosophy of history that claims to say the 'objective' truth of being, but its only content is precisely the consummation of all objective philosophy of history. This paradox seems to be entirely acceptable even for an attitude which is careful not to repeat the errors of metaphysics.

I realize that this argument may appear elusive: a circularity between ontology of weakening and the Christian inheritance, the paradox of a non-metaphysical philosophy that nevertheless believes it possible to speak of Being and its tendency to escape any rigorous definition, law and rule by indefinitely consuming all strong, imposing structures. Yet it is legitimate to suspect that the need for 'clear and distinct ideas' is still an objectivisitic and metaphysical remnant within our mindset. I am not saying that one should accept any statement no matter how vague and contradictory it may be. I am trying to propose arguments, which, even though they do not claim to be definite descriptions of things as they really are, seem to be reasonable interpretations of our condition *here and now*. The rigour of post-metaphysical discourse consists in the effort to cultivate an attitude of persuasion without proclaiming a "universal" viewpoint, which is no viewpoint at all, an attitude that is aware of coming from and addressing someone belonging to the same process, of which it has no neutral vision but risks an interpretation. In this case, a neutral reason is not only impossible but literally senseless, as if one were to try to pull out one's eyes in order to see things objectively.

Secularization: a purified faith?

In the same way, I am conscious that the Christianity I have found again, as the basic text of the transcription proposed by weak ontology, is merely the form of Christianity as it appears (to me, to 'us', to my contemporaries as well) in the epoch of the end of metaphysics. Yet is not Christianity, Jesus' teaching and his interpretation of the prophets, something definitive, a doctrine that is taught authoritatively once and for all, which presents itself as such for our rediscovery? One, indeed, in which the principal sense of secularization as a 'positive' fact within the Christian tradition is precisely the denial of this objectivistic image of return. Secularization as a 'positive' fact signifying the dissolution of the sacral structures of Christian society, the transition to an ethics of autonomy, to a lay state, to a more flexible literalism in the interpretation of dogmas and precepts, should be understood not as the failure of or departure from Christianity, but as a fuller realization of its truth, which is, as we recall, the kenosis, the abasement of God, which undermines the 'natural' features of divinity.

A particularly striking example, for those who are familiar with Italian history, is the destruction of the Popes' temporal power in the nineteenth century; this was interpreted at first as a sacrilege worthy of excommunication, but later acknowledged, at least by shrewder religious minds as a 'liberation' of the proper Christian core of the Church and the affirmation of its authentic image, and was implicitly accepted by the ecclesiastical hierarchy. Taking a look at recent Italian history, the same could be said about the end of what has been called the Church's 'collateralismo' (though hardly anybody remembers the word) in its relations with the Christian Democrats: this transformation, which seemed at first to be an abandonment, loss and impoverishment of the (presence of the) religious sensibility at the political level, is among the events that made possible the end of anticlericalism in Italy and thus prepared the new conditions for listening to the teaching of the Catholic Church. Yet these are merely contingent and mundane examples. Twentieth-century theological literature has plenty of reflections on secularization as the purification of the Christian faith, the progressive dissolution of the 'natural' religious attitude in favour of a more open recognition of faith's authentic essence. It is true that this recognition has often been confused with dialectical theology's assertion of God's absolute transcendence with respect to human aspirations, that is, in terms of an absolute, threatening, bizarre, and 'naturalistic' image of the divine.[10]

Thus, despite the analogies, my own reading of secularization as the path of Christianity's positive development within history is diametrically opposed to that of dialectical theology: secularization does not lead to an increasingly full illumination of God's transcendence, which purifies faith of its too close relationship with time, the aspiration of human perfection, and the illusion regarding the enlightenment of reason. Rather, secularization is the way in which kenosis, having begun with the incarnation of Christ, but even before that with the covenant between God and 'his' people, continues to realize itself more and more clearly by furthering the education of mankind concerning the overcoming of originary violence essential to the sacred and to social life itself.

Revelation continues

From this perspective, it is not scandalous to conceive biblical revelation as an ongoing history in which we are implicated, which is not presented to us as the 'rediscovery' of a core doctrine given once and for all as always the same (accessible in the teaching of the priestly hierarchy, its authorized custodian). Revelation does not speak of an objective truth, but of an ongoing salvation. Moreover,

---

[10] Dialectical theology or theology of crisis was a movement of thought inaugurated in Protestant theology by Karl Barth's commentary on Romans (1919; *The Epistle to the Romans*, trans. E. C. Hoskyns, Oxford: Oxford University Press, 1968), which included Friedrich Gogarten among its members. The terms 'crisis' and 'dialectic' allude to the fact that there is no continuity between divine and human reality, but an infinite qualitative gap that can be bridged only by God's grace, which indeed saves humanity but only after having somehow annihilated it.

this can already be seen in the relationship Jesus established with the Old Testament prophets: he presents himself as the authentic interpretation of prophecies, even though before leaving his disciples he promises to send the Spirit of Truth upon them, which will continue to teach, and thereby to carry on the history of salvation by reinterpreting the content of Jesus' own doctrines as well. One begins to see here too the sense in which the authoritarianism of the Church – given special force by the attitude of Popes such as Wojtyla – is bound up with metaphysics; not only a specific metaphysics such as the Aristotelianism of Thomas Aquinas, which runs throughout the whole western tradition, but metaphysics in Heidegger's sense, that is, the idea that there is an objective truth of Being which once recognized (by reason, enlightened by faith), becomes the stable basis of dogmatic theology and above all of moral teaching, which claims to be grounded upon the eternal nature of things.

The history of salvation and the history of interpretation are much more closely tied to each other than Catholic orthodoxy concedes. It is not just in order to be saved that one needs to hear, understand and apply correctly the evangelical teachings in one's own life. Salvation unfolds in history also by way of an increasingly 'truer' interpretation of Scripture not unlike the relationship between Jesus and the Old Testament: 'you heard it was said . . . but I tell you . . .' And above all, 'I no longer call you servants but friends.' The guiding thread of Jesus' interpretation of the Old Testament is the new and more profound relation of charity established between God and humanity, and consequently between human beings themselves. Salvation is an event in which kenosis, the abasement of God, is realized more and more fully and so undermines the wisdom of the world, the metaphysical dreams of natural reason which conceive God as absolute, omnipotent and transcendent, as

ipsum esse (metaphysicum) subsistens. In this light, secularization
– the progressive dissolution of the natural sacred – is the
very essence of Christianity.

Christianity and modernity

A first consequence of considering secularization as the very
essence of Christianity will be the transformation of the
Christian conception of modernity and the re-enforcement
of a parallel modification of the philosophical perspective on
modern civilization. Indeed, in our century the latter has
been dominated by the 'apocalyptic' implications of the
early twentieth-century existentialist critique, which, as we
have seen, also inspired the Heideggerian polemic against
metaphysics. For philosophy, it is a question of defending
the freedom, historicity and ultimately the finitude of human
existence against the consequences of a radical extension to
all spheres of life of the metaphysical – that is, techno-
scientific – attitude. However, precisely by reflecting on the
roots of the metaphysical attitude in works that followed the
so-called 'turn' in his thinking, Heidegger discovered that
the human subjectivity that was to be defended against the
total organization prepared and promoted by techno-science
is itself deeply complicit with metaphysics insofar as it
believes its own rights may be upheld in the name of a stable
essence (once again 'objective'), which is just another aspect
of the world of essences from which techno-scientific objectivism springs. For Heidegger, the human – humanist –
subject that has to be protected from the pernicious effects
of the total organization is only the 'subject of the object'
or, in other words, the Christian-bourgeois subject who has
constructed the world of the will to power and now

withdraws, frightened, before the consequences of its own action.[11]

Existential philosophy's hostility to the techno-scientific world is inspired by the need to defend an idea of the human essence that can no longer hold once one recognizes the necessity of finding a way out of metaphysics precisely in the name of the freedom and historicity of existence. On the basis of these reflections, Heidegger acknowledges (at least in some rare pages of his work) that the way out of metaphysics might be prepared by the dissolution of subjectivity taking place in this technological society.[12] By contrast, much twentieth-century thought remains bound to a demonizing vision of technological society.

In short: early twentieth century 'humanistic' thought was rightly concerned to oppose the incipient total organization of society that stood out as the effect of techno-scientific mastery. It was precisely in the name of this need that Heidegger criticized the objectivism of metaphysics and recognized its nihilistic outcome. However, the critique of metaphysics also led Heidegger to recognize the deep complicity of the "modern subject" (for example, the individual owner or the subject who believes its conscience to be the ultimate locus of truth and value) with objectivistic metaphysics. This recognition led Heidegger to consider the

[11] For a fuller discussion of these themes, I refer the reader to two of my books: *Introduzione a Nietzsche* (Rome and Bari: Laterza, 1994); and *Introduzione a Heidegger* (Rome and Bari: Laterza, 1993).

[12] I am referring, for example, to the famous *Identity and Difference* (1957), where Heidegger acknowledges in the world of the total organization by modern techno-science the first possible announcement of a new, non-metaphysical relationship between man and Being. It is possible to develop the radically anti-metaphysical interpretation of Heidegger's thought precisely by starting with such texts, on the basis of which arises 'weak thought'. On this difficult theme in Heidegger's thought, cf. ch. 10 of my *The End of Modernity*, trans. Jon Snyder (Baltimore: Johns Hopkins University Press, 1991) and *The Transparent Society*, trans. David Webb (Cambridge: Polity Press, 1992), pp. 55ff.

social transformations that seem to threaten modern subjectivity as possible (we stress this) *chances* of emancipation from
metaphysics. In concrete terms, this means asking whether
the dissolution of subjectivity that takes place in mass society,
and above all in our society of generalized communication,
is not also an occasion for 'salvation' in the sense of the
evangelical expression: whoever would not lose his soul, will
not save it.

Thus we return to secularization as the essence of
modernity and of Christianity itself. From the religious point
of view, the threat presented to the subject by techno-
scientific society lies in the dissolution of sacral values in an
increasingly materialistic, consumerist and Babel-like world,
wherein different systems of values might intersect and
coexist, so as to make a 'true' morality apparently impossible,
and where the play of interpretations (once again, in the
Babel of the mass media) might seem to make any access to
the truth impossible. All this, too, carries the name of
secularization; and from the point of view of the hypothesis
I put forth here, the feature of kenosis in which the history
of salvation is realized must be attributed to this whole
experience of 'dissolution', or of the weakening of strong
structures.

I am deliberately putting forth this idea in scandalous and
provocative terms. In my view, this is necessary in order to
shake the religious and the philosophical habit of taking for
granted the threat of modernization to values, authenticity,
freedom and so on. Insofar as Christianity is concerned –
above all Roman Catholicism – one can understand the
meaning and importance of all this by recalling that many of
the conflicts which have characterized the life of the Church
in modernity – and perhaps much earlier – arose in relation
to the problem of defending the authentic doctrine, which
was always the oldest, as well as of defending doctrinal and
practical features that clearly reflected the links with the

culture of a specific historical world, which was wrongly conceived to be the only one in agreement with evangelical teaching. Without going back to condemnation of Galileo, the Church's opposition to modern democracy illustrates clearly that the recurrent problem in the history of the Church is the absolutization of some contingent historical horizons, which are claimed to be inseparable from the truth of revelation.

It may be recalled that Wilhelm Dilthey (in a book that Heidegger certainly knew and that probably influenced his own vision of the history of philosophy) suggested that the tendency of the Church to 'misunderstand' the meaning of revelation – due to its links with a given historical reality – sprang from the supplemental role of early Christianity in the late-ancient world, after the fall of the Roman Empire, when in the vacuum of civil institutions Popes and bishops were the only authorities capable of assuring a minimal basis of sociability.[13] But, again, the notion of secularization I defend here does not mean that the Church should proceed towards an increasingly sharp separation of its doctrine from an involvement with history – this, as I said above, seems to be the path followed by a certain dialectical theology and generally by any theology which still conceives metaphysically of an authentic religious experience as an encounter with a transcendence so other that it turns out to be incomprehensible, paradoxical and 'absurd'. On the contrary, if secularization is the essence of the history of salvation – that is, a transformation that 'reduces' the metaphysical-natural sacred by virtue of God's decision to institute a relation of friendship with humanity (this is the meaning of Jesus' incarnation) – then one must oppose the unwarranted linkage of Christian doctrine with this or that given historical

---

[13] Wilhelm Dilthey, *Introduction to the Human Sciences*, ed. Rudolf Makkfreel and Frijhof Rodi (Princeton: Princeton University Press, 1989).

reality with the most complete readiness to read the 'signs of the times', in order that we may always identify ourselves anew with history by honestly recognizing our own historicity. Once again, this is what Jesus did with his reading and 'realization' (itself historical) of the Old Testament prophecies.

Demythification against paradox: the meaning of kenosis

On this basis, then, will it not be easier to draw the perspective of modern reason – generally thought to be inimical to faith – closer to the substance of Christian revelation? As is well known, demythification has been one of the most popular terms in twentieth-century theology – though less so, of course, in Catholic theology, at least in its 'official' version. I have no intention of retrieving it in its original meaning, nor of tracing its history in the recent past.[14] However, it is all too clear that what consistently prevents the average modern man from adhering to Christianity or making the 'choice for faith' – both on the level of dogma and of morals – is precisely the scandalous state of many doctrines and moral positions. The evangelical text seems to need a good dose of demythification, the elimination of myth, to speak intelligibly to contemporary educated man. I am well aware that for good textual reasons, the

[14] This history has been marked above all by Rudolf Bultmann's work. For a general sense of his work, see Rudolf Bultmann, 'The New Testament and Mythology', in *Kerygma and Myth*, ed. Werner Bartsch (New York: Torchbooks, 1961); see also Rudolf Bultmann and Karl Jaspers, *Myth and Christianity: An Inquiry into the Possibility of Religion without Myth* (New York: Noonday Press, 1958).

Christian faith has often been presented as essentially scandalous, as so paradoxical as to demand a 'leap' (take certain passages from St Paul on the scandal of Christ; but perhaps it was a scandal for the Jews, because it did not bring about the Kingdom of Israel).

As I have already mentioned, I have the suspicion – and believe it to be well founded – that all this rhetoric is still deeply bound up with a metaphysical-naturalistic conception of God. The only great paradox and scandal of Christian revelation is the incarnation of God, the kenosis – that is, the removal of all the transcendent, incomprehensible, mysterious and even bizarre features that seem to move so many theorists of the leap of faith. In the name of such a transcendence, it is easy to smuggle in a defence of the authoritarianism of the Church and of its many dogmatic and moral positions, bound up as they are with the absolutization of doctrines and contingent historical events, which have been more or less overcome. All of us should claim the right not to be turned away from the truth of the Gospel in the name of a sacrifice of reason demanded only by a naturalistic, human, all too human, ultimately unchristian, conception of God's transcendence.

Am I trying to substitute an easy Christianity for the harsh and paradoxical one presented by the defenders of the 'leap'? I would say that I am only trying to cling more faithfully than them to Jesus' paradoxical affirmation that we should no longer consider ourselves to be servants of God, but his friends. It is not, therefore, an easy Christianity, but rather a friendly one, just as Christ himself preached it to us.

Demythification of morality

This may be the right place for a brief remark on the
paradoxical aspect of the contemporary 'return' of religion,
in particular Christianity, in our society. Today, for reasons
I tried to untangle at the outset, or perhaps for other ones
which elude me, in countries like (and it is not alone in this)
Italy the Catholic Church's teaching tends to be heard with
more attention and respect. Many 'Christian values' seem to
be more popular than before: there is a general condemnation of racism, a pervasive humanitarianism (sometimes
couched in a rhetoric that makes it sound grotesque) which
rejects the idea of war, which is moved by the Third World's
misery, and calls for peace and solidarity. To be sure, this
does not at all mean that our world is any better in practice
than it was in the past. However, it does have a meaning; in
regard to the specific reality of Italy and the West, it means
that modern anticlericalism, founded on the self-assurance of
scientistic and historicist reason that saw no limit to its
increasingly total domination, has come to an end.

In this climate, it seems that the proclamation of the
Catholic Church, planted squarely in defence of a family
and sexual morality that even practising Catholics no longer
take seriously, appears to seek justification less in doctrinal
principles (which are often simply laughable; for example,
when they seem to identify masturbation with genocide)
than in the need to defend an image of the 'true believer'.
And the latter is to be distinguished from tepid Christians
precisely through a practice of virtue that no reasonable
morality demands, but which serves to strengthen the unity
of the Church conceived almost like an army where soldiers
who are not entirely resolute are not admitted. What I am

trying to say is that the present Pope's insistence on indefensible aspects of Catholic sexual morality (just think of the prohibition on using condoms in the epoch of Aids) seems to be motivated less by fundamental principles (even if one takes up the naturalistic and essentialistic metaphysics preferred by this Pope) than by the desire to avoid the impression that Christian morality and doctrine may be weakening. In short, Christianity must beware of looking too kindly on humanity, on its passions (even those lived legitimately) and on the very demands of life on the planet (I am thinking of the prohibition on setting any limit to birth control at a time of demographic explosion).

The 'easiness' of faith that ensues from the idea of secularization as the very essence of the Christian message of salvation cannot be entirely reduced to the dilution of morality. What is pointlessly scandalous in the Christian message is not only some particularly or primarily 'troubling' aspect of ecclesiastical morality, as one thinking in a realist vein might believe. Moreover, today, aside from the Church's official documents, questions of sexual morality are less central to pastoral practice. The very centrality of sex in life – that centrality for which immorality in contemporary language amounts to an excess or disorder of sexual behaviour – seems to be in decline under the force of the (providential, perhaps) pervasiveness of pornography. One might even ask, following the trajectory of Foucault's later work, whether psychoanalysis itself, in its fixation on sexuality, is not an outdated phenomenon, having arisen in modernity, an epoch that was phobic about sex and thus also obsessed by it. For sex has now become the last sanctuary for consciousness, perhaps on account of the increasingly intense planing and levelling down of all the other aspects of life that no longer escape from the general process of rationalization. But even this is a development which here we can only hint at. What should be taken into consideration, for me, is the hypothesis that even the role of sexuality in individual and social life is implicated in the process of secularization; not because the weakening of traditional religious morality makes sex freer, but above all because sex tends to lose the sacral aura – the nineteenth-century bourgeoisie's paradise and hell – which it has in fact preserved in psychoanalysis.

Demythification of dogmas

In this way, traditional religious morality is not (or need not be) the object of secularization. If it is true that the whole relationship between God and the world must be seen from the perspective of kenosis, that is, of the dilution, weakening and denial of what the natural religious mentality believed to be God, then the Christian vision of God and humanity can face the process of demythification without fear of its essential content being disfigured or lost. In Sunday sermons we should no longer hear educated priests talking of 'that wretch Kant' (a name which for many believers means absolutely nothing), just because his critique of religion made it impossible (or at least philosophically doubtful) to believe in the traditional proofs of the existence of God as the cause of the world's existence. Is it really impossible to listen to Jesus' teaching unless one concedes that it can be demonstrated that God is the cause of the physical world's existence? It is true that the Bible calls God father and creator, but it also calls him shepherd, assigns to him many 'warrior-God' attitudes and makes him share Israel's hatred of its enemies, who at times will be destroyed on his command.

The reader will now expect me to develop this argument concerning the 'absurdity' of the biblical text and the traditional teaching of the Church. But aside from other considerations (my lack of exegetical expertise, various reasons for the difficulty of such an enterprise, which has been in any case abundantly developed by the rationalist and Enlightenment critiques of the Bible), such an aim could only be inspired by the project of accomplishing the demythification of Christianity once and for all from the perspective of reason as the criterion of truth, albeit with the intention not of eliminating it, as the critical rationalists wanted, but rather of tracing it back to its ineliminable, original kernel of truth. Yet, as Jesus taught, the sole truth of Christianity is the one produced again and again through the 'authentication' that occurs in dialogue with history, assisted by the Holy Spirit. We may think that the seventeenth-century Church was wrong in condemning Galileo, but we may think so legitimately only from our historically situated perspective in light of what has happened and of what we have learned in the meantime; but not from the perspective of the eternal truth of Scripture or of science. Accordingly, we cannot conceive the demythification of the Christian message as a definitive undertaking; it may be that this is another meaning of the close relationship between faith and works of which the Bible often speaks: it is only within the history of salvation, guided through different epochs and moments by Providence (according to a rhythm which signifies progress towards the maturity or end of times) that the sense of the evangelical message itself is clarified and acquires meanings that are less and less complicit with the naturalistic religious attitude of the sacred as violence.

What we do know, then, and what becomes clear with the idea of secularization as an essential feature of the history of salvation, is that we cannot or should not allow ourselves to be separated from Jesus' teachings on account of metaphysical prejudice, whether it be developed by scientistic or

historicist mentality which take it to be 'logically' untenable,
or by ecclesiastical authoritarianism which fixes the meaning
of revelation once and for all in the form of irrational myths,
to which we are expected to adhere in the name of God's
absolute transcendence, which is both metaphysical and
violent. Modern religiosity, the only one given us as our
vocation, if it is to be authentic, cannot be set apart from
one of Luther's original teachings: the 'free investigation' of
Scripture. Even though, as I shall argue in a moment, such
an investigation cannot put aside its links with the community of the Church (which is not identical with the
ecclesiastical authority), it remains true that we can no longer
conceive salvation to be hearing and applying of a message
that does not stand in need of interpretation. From the
perspective of religious experience, the actuality of hermeneutics, which with good reason regards itself as *the* philosophy of modernity, means that for us, more than in past
epochs, salvation takes place through interpretation.[15] It is
not only necessary to understand the gospel text in order to
apply it to our existence in practice. Before 'turning to
practice' this comprehension must be identified with the
very history of (our) salvation, and the personal interpretation of Scripture is the first imperative proposed by Scripture
itself.

So what do I rediscover, if and when, led by certain
conclusions elaborated at a philosophical level, but also by
an ensemble of 'cultural' motives that I share with my
world, an inheritance that has not ceased operating in my
existence, I rediscover Christianity? Of course, I do not
face a legacy of clearly defined doctrines and precepts that
would resolve all my doubts and show me clearly what to

---

[15] For a fuller discussion of this point, I refer the reader to my *Beyond Interpretation:
The Meaning of Hermeneutics for Philosophy*, trans. David Webb (Cambridge: Polity
Press, 1996); and the essay 'Verso un'ontologia dell'attualità', in *Filosofia 87*, ed. G.
Vattimo (Rome and Bari: Laterza, 1988).

do. It is true that the Christian doctrine proclaimed by the Catholic Church tends to present itself in this form, such that if then I do not find it, it can only be because deep down I have no intention of discovering the Christian doctrine in its truth. This dogmatic and disciplinary Christianity, however, has nothing to do with what I and my contemporaries 'rediscover'. It is not like this that the teaching of Jesus shows itself capable of addressing us. Is it simply our fault, or should this fact give pause for thought to those who see themselves as the custodians of the truth of faith and of the mission to proclaim it to the world? The Christianity that I or my contemporary 'half'-believers rediscover embraces the official Church as well, but only as part of a more complex event, which includes the question concerning the continuous reinterpretation of the biblical message.

To be plain: what I have rediscovered is a doctrine which has its keystone in the kenosis of God and in salvation understood as the dissolution of the sacred as natural-violent. This doctrine has been passed on to me by an institution, which, as far as I can understand, tends to de-emphasize this kenotic and secularizing core, but not to the point of obscuring it (in the concreteness of the believer's religious experience) or of retreating from any judgement which is passed in its name on the institution itself. For this reason, I insist strongly that 'one should not allow oneself to be moved away from Christ's teaching' because of the scandal caused by the official teaching of the Church. I know well, and many confessors and spiritual directors have repeated it to me, that one should not allow oneself to be scandalized by the Church, or that this scandal too is a test to which God (but is this not always the paradoxical, capricious and unpredictable God of natural religion?) puts me in order to establish the purity of my faith. I can concede that there is a necessity for scandals to occur, but in this case their meaning lies precisely in warning of the necessity of a personal interpretation of Scripture without which Jesus and salvation would remain inaccessible to me.

Secularization: the limit of charity

The attitude of many people towards the Church today undergoes a strange movement of search and disillusionment: one discovers (one's interest in) Christianity and turns to the teaching of the Pope and the bishops. However, soon one moves away once again because this teaching, which claims to be fulfilling its mission by merely reproposing a rigid vision of human nature, does not speak 'words of eternal life'. In addition, the moral teaching derived from it is no longer theoretically tenable. In terms closer to my experience as a philosophical scholar the rediscovery of Christianity is made possible by the dissolution of metaphysics, that is, by the end of objectivistic-dogmatic philosophies as well as of European culture's claim to have discovered and realized the true 'nature' of humanity. This doctrine, bolstered by metaphysical language that can be of appeal only to the reactive and aggressive impulses at work in many of the forms of fundamentalism around which we live, cannot be presented to anyone who has rediscovered Christianity on the basis of these experiences. These experiences, let us repeat it, are had not only by philosophers, but by whoever lives in the pluralism of late-industrial societies. Christianity recovered as the doctrine of salvation (namely, secularizing kenosis), is not a legacy of doctrines defined once and for all, to which one might appeal in seeking solid ground in the sea of uncertainty, the post-metaphysical Babel of languages. However, the critical principle it provides is sufficiently clear to allow one to orient oneself in relation to this world, above all to the Church, and to the process of secularization. If one responds to the question concerning the 'limit' of secularization, this critical principle can be clarified. In fact kenosis can be conceived neither as the indefinite negation of God nor as a justification of any particular interpretation of the sacred Scriptures.

Again, it is necessary to recall the parallelism between a theology of secularization and an ontology of weakening. In the case of weak ontology, the long farewell to the strong structures of Being can only be conceived as an indefinite process of consummation and dissolution of the structures themselves, which does not culminate in 'fully realized nothingness' (the expression itself reveals the contradictory nature of this idea). For even the pure nothingness that awaits us at the end of the history of nihilism, would be an objectively laid out presence. One can only conceive nihilism as a history (even when Nietzsche speaks of an accomplished nihilism, he means a nihilism which is no longer experienced reactively as loss and mourning for the end of metaphysics, but as the *chance* of a new position of man in relation to Being). Is it only a logical reason – the contradiction of thinking nothingness, in place of Being, as a fully laid out metaphysical presence at the end of the process – which compels us to conceive nihilism as an infinite history? Or should we believe that it is precisely the Christian inspiration at work in (this) philosophy which guides thinking in this direction? I do not think one can answer this question, which has come up several times in the course of the argument. At least not if the recognition of weak ontology's relation to (or dependence on) the Christian message calls for the recovery of the true origin; as if, for example, one were to concede that here we are 'passing off' as philosophy a theological discourse which belongs to another genre, with different rules, which cannot claim to count as a philosophical argument. The relation of (this) philosophy to Christian theology comes to light in the context of secularization, which somehow foresees such a philosophical 'transcription' of the biblical message; however, it does not consider such a transcription to be a misunderstanding, a masking or an appearance which must be removed in order to find the originary truth, but rather a legitimate interpretation of the doctrine of the incarnation of God.

If one thinks of nihilism as an infinite history in terms of the religious 'text' that is its basis and inspiration, it will speak of kenosis as guided, limited and endowed with meaning, by God's love.[16] The precept 'Dilige, et quod vis fac' ('Love, and do what you will'), found in the work of St Augustine, expresses clearly the only criterion on the basis of which secularization must be examined. Elsewhere I have observed that the term 'charity' itself has staked an unexpected, but nonetheless significant claim to citizenship in philosophy.[17] Besides all this, which could be another symptom of the return of Christianity, and the sentimental preference for love rather than justice, severity and the majesty of God, it is sufficiently clear that the New Testament orients us to recognize this as the sole, supreme principle.

The interpretation given by Jesus Christ of Old Testament prophecies, or (better) the interpretation which he himself *is*, reveals its true and only meaning: God's love for his creatures. However, this 'ultimate' meaning precisely by virtue of its being *caritas*, is not really ultimate and does not possess the peremptoriness of the metaphysical principle, which cannot be transcended, and before which all question-

[16] Augustine, *In epistulam Johannis ad Parthos*, X. vii. 8.
[17] Cf. the already mentioned *Beyond Interpretation*, p. 40.

ing ceases. Perhaps the reason why nihilism is an infinite, never-ending process lies in the fact that love, as the 'ultimate' meaning of revelation, is not truly ultimate. Moreover, the reason why philosophy at the end of the metaphysical epoch finds it can no longer believe in foundations, in the first cause which is given objectively before the mind's eye, may be that it has become aware (insofar as it has been educated also, if not only, by the Christian tradition) of the implicit violence of every finality, of every principle that would silence all questioning.[18]

Enlightenment rediscovered

As one can see, I am simply trying to unfold, in a comprehensive and hopefully persuasive manner what was for me the significance of the 'rediscovery' of the nexus between weak ontology and secularization as the positive meaning of Christian revelation. This discovery provides me not only with a unitary perspective from which to view the epoch in which I live: the history of modernity, the meaning of social rationalization, of technology; it also paves the way for a renewed dialogue with the Christian tradition, to which I have always belonged (as the rest of modernity), yet whose meaning has become incomprehensible to me, led astray (scandalized, literally: obstacles placed in my path) by the metaphysical rigidity of the philosophical mindset of modernity and of the Church's dogmatic and disciplinary narrow-mindedness.

[18] The only possible philosophical definition of violence seems to be the silencing of all questioning by the authoritative peremptoriness of the first principle; cf. my essay 'Metaphysics, Violence, and Secularization', in *Recoding Metaphysics: The New Italian Philosophy*, ed. Giovanna Borradori (Evanston: Northwestern University Press, 1988).

In particular, given that I intend here to address the question of religion, the idea of secularization as an indefinite drift limited only by the principle of charity allows me to avoid the impasse in which modern consciousness always finds itself when confronted by Christian revelation: the impossibility of adhering to a doctrine that appears too sharply contrasted with the 'conquests' of enlightened reason, too full of myths which demand to be unmasked. If, in the wake of the philosophical critique of the metaphysical attitude, I seriously try to understand the meaning of kenosis, I realize that Christ himself is the unmasker, and that the unmasking inaugurated by him (or of which he shows the true meaning of unmasking, insofar as kenosis begins with creation itself and the Old Testament) is the meaning of the history of salvation itself.[19] Then to believe in salvation will not mean adhering to the letter of everything that is written in the Gospel and in the dogmatic teaching of the Church, but rather in trying to understand the meaning of the evangelical text for me, here, now. In other words, reading the signs of the times with no other provision than the commandment of love, which cannot be secularized, because (if you will) it is a 'formal' commandment, not unlike Kant's categorical imperative, which does not command something specific once and for all, but rather applications that must be 'invented' in dialogue with specific situations and in light of what the holy Scriptures have revealed.

Yet, will unmasking, which modern reason felt obliged to apply to the revelation, not also be applied to the idea of revelation itself, that is, to the idea of divine intervention in history? And to the idea of creation, of humanity's depen-

---

[19] One could read in this way what is written in bk 1, ch. 3 of Thomas à Kempis, *The Imitation of Christ* (New York: Random House, 1984), p. 6: 'Cui aeternum loquitur, a multis opinionibus expeditur' ('He whom the eternal Word teaches is set free from a multitude of theories').

dence upon divinity and so forth? How shall I reconcile the rediscovery of Christianity, even via kenosis as secularization, with this radical unmasking? I can only give two answers to this question, which are not, for me, logically conclusive, but are sufficiently persuasive. First of all: as far as I know twentieth-century theology has welcomed aspects of unmasking in modernity as the secularized 'authentication' of faith. I am thinking here of Dietrich Bonhoeffer's notion of a Christianity come of age, which in his view should no longer see God as the supreme *deus ex machina* that is to resolve every problem and conflict, and the many theoretical positions that, in the light of the Holocaust of the Jews under Nazism, have been taken with regard to the possibility of thinking God not as omnipotent, but as in struggle alongside humanity for the triumph of goodness.

What I hope to illustrate by way of these examples – to which others may be added that are perhaps still more persuasive – is that if one reflects without appealing to metaphysical prejudices – which assume that the existence and essential attributes of God may be demonstrated once and for all, and the principles of 'natural' law derived from them down to the most detailed prescription for individual and social life, including even the prohibition of condoms, there is cogent reason for not trying to understand the Christian meaning (kenotic, secularizing and desacralizing in the positive sense) of the most radical of modern demythifications, provided they too abandon any claim to metaphysical absoluteness, by which they have all too often been inspired. In other words, having left behind the metaphysical claim to objectivity, today none should be able to say, 'God does not exist', or that God's nature and existence have been rationally determined once and for all. What, I believe, can be said in non-metaphysical thinking is that a great part of the theoretical and practical conquests of reason in modernity, up to the rational organization of society, to liberalism and democracy, is rooted in the Judaeo-Christian tradition, and cannot be conceived outside it.

Once we see that this matter cannot be judged from an 'external', absolute and suprahistorical perspective, it is reasonable to approach it by formulating an interpretation. As Luigi Pareyson would say, one should grasp the internal rule of the process, as if it were like the meaning of an itinerary in which we are implicated, and which comprises indications to be borne in mind in our own judgements and choices.[20] 'To grasp' the rule of the process in which we are implicated does not mean to look at it objectively and to demonstrate it as uniquely true: this is why one speaks here of interpretation. Another reason to recover Christianity, apart from the (interpretative) recognition of our belonging to this tradition, is that Christian doctrine 'fore-sees' inter-pretation and fore-sees the history of Being in its interpreta-tive (kenotic) universal character.[21]

The substance of faith

All this leads to the second response I mentioned a moment ago. The 'discovery' that secularization is the sense of the history of salvation is not advanced as an essential, metaphys-ical statement. Rather, this interpretation of the history of

[20] Pareyson is perhaps the only one, among the hermeneutical thinkers who formulates an explicit theory of the interpretative act that does not confine itself to the recovery of Dilthey's notion of 'understanding'. On this, cf. his *Estetica: teoria della formatività* (1950; Milan: Bompiani, 1988), especially ch. 5; and the essay on 'La conoscenza degli altri', in *Esistenza e persona* (1950; Genoa: Il Melangolo, 1985), especially pp. 210ff.

[21] Translators' note: Vattimo uses the verb 'to fore-see' following Heidegger's usage of the word '*Vor-sicht*', fore-sight, which means to have an anticipatory pre-thematic vision (of Being).

Being as weakening and its relation to Christian revelation appears (the most) reasonable and the strongest precisely from our point of view in late modernity. Yet to remain at the level of premises, or by way of introduction: having grasped the principle of secularization by which I can again listen to the substance of biblical revelation, and having identified the commandment of charity as the limit of the secularizing 'transcription', how shall I relate myself in practice to what is called religion, Christianity, faith, and Christian morality? Shall I go back to church – to the practice of sacraments and to the sermons in Sunday Mass – and take the Pope's encyclical letters as guides for my job as philosopher, and as part-time observer and critic of contemporary culture, which I take to be identical with my job as philosopher?

Since I have been speaking in the first person here, accepting the risks involved by such a choice, I confess that, until now, I have returned to church only on sad or formal occasions (though not merely out of formality): funerals of people who were dear to me, or baptisms and weddings. A few times, and for primarily aesthetic reasons (which I am careful not to undervalue or even to distinguish from the 'authentic' religious ones), I have been to the Latin sung Christmas liturgy in one of few churches that still celebrate it. I no longer profess the disdain I once felt, as a fervent Catholic, for half-believers (a verse of the gospel says that those who are lukewarm in their belief will be thrown up), those people who go to church merely for weddings, baptisms, and funerals. It seems, rather, that everything I have said so far comes down to a defence of the half-believers.

The Italian title of this book (*Credere di credere*) expresses exactly this defence. It has been going round in my head for many years, since one hot afternoon I made a telephone call, from an ice-cream shop near a bus stop in Milan, to Gustavo

Bontadini, a distinguished representative of 'neoclassical' Aristotelian-Thomistic philosophy. Although I did not share his theoretical theses, I felt bound to him by deep affection and admiration. The call was about the competitive examination for a university chair. As we were both members in the examining commission, we had some confidential academic business to discuss. But while we were still greeting each other, Bontadini, with whom I had not spoken for a long time, shifted to fundamental matters, asking me suddenly whether at bottom I still believed in God. I don't know whether my response was conditioned by the paradoxical situation in which the question arose: next to the telephone was a table of women, eating ice cream and drinking orange juice in the heat. So I answered that I believed that I believed.

Since then that answer seems the best formulation of my relationship with religion, with the Christian Catholic tradition in which I have grown up, and which remains the point of reference of my reflections on religion. Once again one might ask why I privilege the reference to Christianity. In part, I have already explained why the rediscovery of religion, for me, has to do with Christianity, at least as a point of departure. The reason is that in Christianity I find the original 'text' of which weak ontology is the transcription. And I probably arrived at this formulation of ontology, because it was from those Christian roots that I began. Hence, I run up against a circle, the relative contingency of the whole. So what? Anyone who finds this argument outrageous should take it upon himself to prove the contrary, which could only be a renewed metaphysical position, and so, all in all, somewhat unlikely.

The moral question

When, as a fervent, even militant Catholic, I felt disdain for half-believers, I thought I knew that the problem of religious practice for many of them had to do less with the rational untenability of Christian dogmas than with the rejection of the ethics proclaimed by the Church. In particular, I thought that half-believers were intolerant of the sixth command-ment and of Catholic sexual morality. Most of my friends from the *liceo* (secondary school) had abandoned religious practice because they did not want to submit themselves to Christian discipline in matters of sexuality. I do not know whether that is still the case nowadays: though the Church's official teaching and the principles of 'natural' morality, which have led the Pope to prohibit the use of condoms in the period of Aids, are still the same, it is widely known that the pastoral practice of spiritual confessors is far more toler-ant. Yet, for someone who goes to church while having no intention of renouncing the 'sinful life' in which, according to official ecclesiastical teaching, he lives, the situation remains embarrassing and counter to all personal dignity, consistency and transparency.

In all likelihood, sexual morality is no longer the primary route leading to the denial of God, as it was for teenagers growing up in the 1950s. But back then it was so, and it would be silly to deny that problems of this kind had any role in my moving away from religious practice. To make this confession less trivial, I might add that during my adolescence sexual morality was never preached or presented to me in threatening terms or as the main issue. This was, perhaps, due to the confessors and spiritual directors I happened to have and to whom I still feel very grateful. In fact, the most heated discussions I had with my confessor, a distinguished Thomist of exceptional humanity and intelligence, were about Catholic politics in Italy, and more generally about 'the just war', a theme that has sadly come up again, and one that demonstrates the tendency of the Church to arrive at a compromise with power.

The issue of just war seemed to entail the idea, characteristic of my confessor's Thomistic perspective, that Christian truth is based on natural metaphysics (the proof of God's existence, the laws of nature, etc.), an idea that I found untenable. The question of natural law mattered to me for reasons that were both philosophical (I had begun to read Nietzsche) and personal. (Is the motto 'cherchez la femme' ultimately true? I do not give much credence to it, though it would not be a problem for me to acknowledge it. The woman, or indeed, any object of love for the sake of which someone might decide not to go to Mass any longer, is precisely a matter of love. I am not at all sure that this love (*eros*) has nothing to do with the *agape* (*caritas*) proclaimed by the gospel.) The second, perhaps more radical, reason why the question of natural law was important for me was that I had realized (would it not be *politically correct* to say that I had chosen?) that I was a member of a sexual minority that engaged in what, according to Catholic catechism, was a vice against nature, a sin against the Holy Spirit, or something of the kind.

I certainly did not make this discovery or choice because I had spent time in Catholic circles, as someone might maliciously think: colleges, seminaries and convents have often been held to be places where homosexual habits develop, but I was never aware of it myself. I could not believe it then, and certainly do not believe now, that homosexual behaviour is intrinsically immoderate, so that a morally worthy life could be found only in the legitimate 'usage' of sexuality for reproduction. Today I realize, more clearly than then, that the abhorrence of the Catholic Church for homosexuality is one of the most superstitious remnants that underscore the Church, as if one were to proclaim that there are impure animals, contact with which must be avoided at any cost; or as in the case of the Pope's anti-feminism, which leads him to dismiss the idea of women's priesthood, solely on the basis that all the apostles were male (but, as someone has pointed out, the apostles were fishermen, Jews, and married; should not this matter?), which is interpreted as providential in the light of a meta-physical conception of woman's 'natural' vocation.

I stopped going to church when, on the one hand, in the course of my study of philosophy I came across more and more reasons pointing to the untenability of 'Christian metaphysics', and when, on the other, at the personal level I tried to live the life of my sentiments free from the neurotic schema of sin and confession. Moreover, how could I belong to a Church that treated me, in its public teaching, as morally despicable, or, if I accepted this title, as a sick person in need of healing, a monstrous brother who must be loved but kept hidden? It is true that the question of homosexual-ity concerns a specific group of people that remains a minority in the Church. However, for me (as for others, and I am thinking of the way that Pasolini lived his homo-sexuality) this question has become the key for interpreting all the other superstitions within the Church, and all the forms of social exclusion outside it.

One may of course put less emphasis on the problem of one's homosexuality by refusing to become an obsessed professional of gay liberation. Yet not to the point of ignoring the relation between this and other forms of exclusion that profoundly mark our society and, by implication, the church, which seems to have condemned itself, in matters of morality and politics, to always being centuries late regarding the evolution of manners. It may be that Pasolini's view of himself as emblematic of all the rejected of the earth, a sort of latter-day Jesus Christ put on the cross by every manner of Pharisee, is outdated now. But in the end for me, and for others like me, to have lived my condition of sexual alienation as one that is bound up with other forms of racial or class alienation or exclusion has been of decisive significance: it has led me to discover an interpretative key that I would never renounce, in spite of its evident limitations. The fact that I place less emphasis on Pasolini's model or on certain revolutionary excesses of the 1960s and the 1970s, is closely linked to the idea of secularization. I am not convinced that truth resides at the margins, that there is an ideal proletariat (whether or not it is, or is any longer, Marxist) that carries the authentic meaning of history, to which the alienated minority of homosexuals would belong. But I do know that the abhorrence for this type of 'deviation' is a manifestation of the violence bound up with the natural sacred that Christ's incarnation calls me to eliminate, along with other forms of violence, and by means that in turn are untainted by the same sin. For the love of my neighbour, and to avoid becoming a violent opponent of violence, I could even give up hoping that in a definitive discussion I might change the minds of many people, with whom I might otherwise agree on many themes and who are at most tolerant of my style of life, without entirely approving it. But I cannot believe that one should compromise certain principles and fundamental rights, least of all at the level of state laws (for example, gays' rights to have families acknowledged by the state, now denied by the lay state in the name of a metaphysical conception of the 'natural' family which is espoused only by the Catholic Church). The point is to regard the reduction of violence no longer as an ideal condition of authenticity to be realized once and for all by corresponding to the eternal essence of humanity, morality and society, but as an ongoing process.

To return where?

From this digression, which centres too much around the first person (an additional risk accepted for the sake of the literary genre), one may at least understand that I have no intention, with the rediscovery of Christianity, of placing my life in order on the basis of official Catholic morality. Above all, returning to the question of doctrine, it is not, for me (or for anyone who has a similar trajectory through secularization in modernity), a matter of rediscovering the literality of the truths of faith as they are often so preached by the Church. I am persuaded, and not merely out of attachment to my passions, that if I have a vocation to recover Christianity, it will consist in the task of rethinking revelation in secularized terms in order to 'live in accord with one's age', therefore in ways that do not offend my culture as, to a greater or lesser extent, a man who belongs to his age. This is the exact opposite of returning to the father's house (as a Catholic discipline), filled with repentance, prepared to abase oneself and to mortify one's intellectual pride.

Let me repeat that I am merely defending the right to hear the word of the gospel again, without being obliged to share in the outright superstitions that obscure the official doctrine of the Church in philosophical and moral matters. I want to interpret the word of the gospel as Jesus taught us, by translating the often violent letter of precepts and prophecies into a language more concordant with the supreme commandment of charity.

I return briefly to the example of the Pope's stubborn rejection of the female priesthood: the metaphysical superstition that women possess a natural role which excludes the possibility of priesthood is clearly against the duty of charity, which consists in acknowledging the new awareness of women in our society. I am not defending women's 'natural' right to the priesthood, opposing one metaphysics to another. I am just saying that the recognition of 'new' rights, the attention given to all the movements dedicated to raising awareness that lead to a reduction in objective violence against people are matters of charity; this attention should not be impeded by the belief in objective metaphysical structures, a belief that lends itself inevitably to superstition and idolatry.

The examples of a female priesthood and of the taboo of homosexuality are an easy ground for the application of my argument about secularization. What about all the other cases where superstitious language survives within Christian doctrine? In the final analysis, if the Pope will not grant the priesthood to women, it is because the Bible calls God father and not mother, though even the Bible does set aside an important role for the Virgin Mary. Are the fatherhood of God, the 'family' structure of the Trinity, Mary's being a virgin mother and other substantial elements of Christian revelation all to be secularized and demythified? It is true that in charity I have a general principle that can set a limit to secularization. But one might ask how this principle could or should be applied in practice. If I say that I believe that I believe, what exactly do I believe about Christian doctrine, as it has been passed on to us?

A reduced faith

I consider myself a half-believer because I cannot answer this question conclusively. To be sure, I do have some answers, but not of the kind that might allow me to reformulate the Creed in secular terms. For example, I would say that the 'kenotic' interpretation of the articles of faith goes hand in hand with the life of every person, that is, with the commitment to transform them into concrete principles that are incarnate in one's own existence, and irreducible to a formula. Besides, the Creed is above all an external 'symbol' by which members of a community identify themselves, a kind of code, an 'identity card', destined to function as a sign of recognition. True, if one reflects on the bloody struggles over a single term of the Creed, over a single word of Scripture, that have marked the history of Christianity, my interpretation might appear unrealistic; or, rather, perhaps, it may find here its justification by leading us to appreciate that one should not think of the words of Scripture as something over which one might struggle and ultimately kill. Once again, the essence of revelation is reduced to charity, while all the rest is left to the non-finality of diverse historical experiences, even of mythologies that at the time appeared to be 'binding' to particular historical humanities.

If I recite the Creed or if I pray, the words that I employ do not possess, for me, the realistic quality attributed to them by those who hold a metaphysically conceived faith. Accordingly, if I call God 'father', I will freight this term with an ensemble of references tied to my historical experience and to my own biography, which are not indifferent to the problem of attributing human characteristics to div-

inity, not to mention those which are bound up with a
particular model of the family. Of course, if I reflect on all
this, I no longer know what I am saying when I recite the
Lord's Prayer. But it seems to me that this disorientation
also belongs to my experience of faith as well, insofar as it is
a response to kenosis's revelation. Is what Schleiermacher
called the pure feeling of dependence the only sense left in
the use of the term 'father'? Probably yes, and once again
this is the kernel that, in my view, cannot be an object of
reduction or demythification; I am not sure why, but it is
certain that my entire argument concerning the overcoming
of metaphysics − which has led me no longer to speak of
Being as the eternal structure − leads me to think of Being
as event, and accordingly, as something begun by an initiative that is not mine. The historicity of my existence is
provenance, and emancipation − salvation or redemption −
consists in recognizing that Being is event, a recognition that
enables me to enter actively into history, instead of passively
contemplating its necessary laws. Once again, this is the
meaning of the statement 'I no longer call you servants but
friends.'

But is the substance of the Christian tradition that I
recover via weak ontology and the idea of secularization to
be reduced entirely to charity? Do I 'merely' believe that
God loves and creates the world out of love, and that
creatures are called upon for a commitment to charity by
way of response? It is true that, in the gospel, the whole law
and the prophets are reduced to the commandment: 'Love
God above all things, and your neighbour as yourself.' What
will be the meaning, for me, of the stories told in the
Scriptures, and of all the interpretations that have been given
of them in the history of Christian spirituality? There is
some truth, I think, in the reductive outcome of this
argument. Biblical revelation, freighted with myths, is
directed solely towards our education, and the meaning of

this is the love of God and of our neighbour. The same sense may be given to the beautiful *incipit* to Paul's letter to the Hebrews, 'Multifariam et multis modis olim Deus locutus patribus in prophetis . . .' ('In many and various ways God spoke of old to our fathers by the prophets, but in these last days he has spoken to us by a Son'),[22] which is included in the liturgy of one of the three Christmas Masses. However, against the case of pure reduction, the fact remains that Jesus did not think of himself as the final and conclusive unveiling of prophecies, and promised to send the spirit of truth so that revelation could continue. The stories and myths of the Bible have this same sense of incarnation, and, before that, of creation, at least when viewed from the perspective of the Christian faith. They are ways in which the divine Being expresses itself beyond itself by reducing and abasing itself for the sake of love. To be sure, this is a myth, it is the Christian 'explanation' of history, and a difficult one, since it would be impossible for a divine Being that was fully complete in itself to justify any history, not just the myths of Scripture but creation as well.

Yet, what if the act of faith that God demands of us were to consist in the recognition that the commandment of charity is the sole content of the myths of Scripture, of the history of spirituality and Christian theology? Would this amount to saying that once we discover ultimate truth, the commandment of charity, these myths and this history will have no meaning for us? As if one were to say that there is no point in reading the signs of the times, as the gospel calls us to do, since we already know that God's providence and redemptive will are revealed in them. In the same way as charity cannot work in the abstract but must be applied to concrete situations, it is possible that the meaning of revelation may be given to us only within the historical context

---

[22] Hebrews, 1:1.

where we live. Perhaps, we must recognize that the truth of Christianity is secularization in this sense too: Christ's message does not resound in empty space but rather sets a task with respect to the situation in which we find ourselves, which has itself to be defined in recognizable terms, to be understood in the light of charity. The attitude of the believer towards this specific content, however, is on the whole oriented towards demythification, and is therefore, in a certain sense, reductive; but not to the point of working as if from the outside. The demythifying secularization that faith calls us to accomplish with respect to 'history' – from the inherited myths to spirituality, from the writings of the Church fathers to contemporary writings, and so on – is always historically defined as well as engaged; accordingly, secularization is indebted to other mythologies and stories from which it does not prescind, as it cannot put aside its own specific singularity.

Secularization versus tragic thought

Perhaps, in the end it is indeed charity that compels us not to forget the many stories that have been passed on to us, of which we are the heirs, at least insofar as they constitute our provenance. As far as I am concerned, despite my impatience with the scandalously superstitious character of much of the official teaching of today's Church, my disposition towards the Christian tradition is on the whole friendly, marked by gratitude, respect and admiration. I do not allow myself to be outraged by the Crusades or the Inquisition, because they are less my concern than is the fundamentalism of John Paul II. I am sympathetic towards the history of the Christian saints – the martyrs, the virgins, the confessors – told, often as though it were a thing of legend, in the Roman breviary. It is a tradition from which I do not feel the need to free myself, as I do not feel the need to free myself from the traces – which, I hope, are substantial – of my Christian Catholic upbringing. It is a tradition from which I have learned to organize my life, to examine my conscience, to work seriously (when I have managed), in other words, not to be distracted; I concede that my upbringing has been less mystical than moral (and, perhaps, political), tied as it is to a specific moment in the history of Italian Catholicism. I feel deeply bound, in many senses, to the latter, not least because it was delimited by the Church's involvement in the social and political events of contemporary Italy. I am the child of an epoch when faith, for many militant Italian Catholics, was gauged by political events, questions such as the opening to left-wing politics, the nationalization of electric energy, the right (Christian Democratic) or left (Communist) unions. These are all questions that, today, seem to have little relation to the issue of faith; but, once again, a trace of all this is present and alive in my emphasis on secularization, which is diametrically opposed to the widespread apocalyptic or Dostoevskian Christianity of today. While I still have a deep respect for the latter (I am thinking above all of Luigi Pareyson, my mentor), it seems to me to be the last great metaphysical misunderstanding of Christian thought; that is, the idea that there is a radical separation between the history of salvation and secular history by virtue of which the meaning of revelation would be exclusively apocalyptic: the unveiling of the senselessness of world history in light of an event so other that the times and rhythms of history can only have a negative sense, to be annulled in the paradox of the leap of faith, or treated as a time of trial.

Let me try to clarify the meaning and content of the Christianity I recover via the doctrine of secularization by comparing its tonality with that of apocalyptic and tragic

Christianity. Perhaps, the historical and cultural reasons for discovering religion, which I tried to illustrate at the outset of the book, account for the popularity of the tragic and apocalyptic image of Christianity today. This image too is an effect of the end of metaphysics, at least in the sense that it does not regard religion as the summit of a ladder that traverses the objective order of beings and reaches ultimately to the supreme Being, to God. The objective world order has fallen to pieces both because the traditional realistic image of knowledge (according to which the mind is a mirror faithfully reflecting things as they really are 'out there') did not stand up to philosophical critique, and because the will to power has established itself as the sole essence of techno-science, so that if there is a world order, it is produced by man, by his intellect or praxis. Although God is no longer conceived as the supreme point of the objective world order, his transcendence is nonetheless re-affirmed: for religious consciousness God appears as the 'wholly other' of which much contemporary philosophy speaks, and who becomes present in our experience primarily through 'catastrophic' events, in that they put all the certainties and reassurances that can be formed by means of our human tools into crisis. In the twentieth century the philosophy of religion has been primarily 'existentialist': whereas Thomas Aquinas and the medieval age sought to prove the existence of God by means of the world order, modern religious thought has looked to the precarious and tragic nature of the human condition to find its proof of God. To be sure, it finds plenty of material for its own reflection in the many sensational 'failures' of modern reason: on the one hand Auschwitz, on the other the destructiveness of Eurocentric colonialism have rendered the ideology of progress untenable. Today a number of contradictions in techno-science, from ecological devastation to the most recent problems in bioethics, seem to force everybody to acknowledge that 'by now only a God can save us', as Heidegger said in a famous interview given toward the end of his life, and published posthumously.[23]

It will be clear by now that the question I want to raise against this tragic and apocalyptic Christianity – whose only claim to truth requires the radical devaluation of world history – is that it is merely the equally unacceptable inversion of the Christianity that believed that it could legitimize itself via traditional metaphysics. Here one not only does not make any step forward in relation to the metaphysical religious nature of the past, but rather one makes a step backward. What is more authentically 'Christian', that is, farther removed from the capricious and violent deity of the natural religions: God as the supreme ground of reality, as found in Graeco-Christian metaphysics, or the wholly other of tragic religiosity inspired by existentialist thought?

If we consider the meaning of creation and redemption to be kenosis, as I believe we must in the light of the gospel, we will probably have to concede that the continuity of God and the world established by classical metaphysics is more authentically 'kenotic' than the transcendence attributed to God in naming him 'the wholly other'. Despite its apparent 'heterodoxy' – since the official teaching of the Church is basically inspired by the Aristotelian-Thomistic tradition, however diluted or disguised in form – this tragic Christianity is, objectively, profoundly attuned with Catholicism's most fundamentalist aspects, as represented by Pope John Paul II. However, these implications are only the most visible signs of tragic Christianity's overall regressive character, which is inspired primarily by the Old Testament faith, and which tends to undervalue the meaning of Christ's incarnation itself; one views the incarnation as the condition

---

[23] Heidegger, 'Nur ein Gott kann uns retten', *Der Spiegel*, 31 May 1976.

of death upon the cross, a death which testifies to God's paradoxical transcendence and alterity with respect to any mundane logic.

There is a sort of predominance of Judaic religiosity in the return of religion into contemporary thought (let me make clear that this observation has no anti-semitic intention whatsoever). It is a fact that the total otherness of God with respect to the world appears to be affirmed at the expense of any recognition of novelty in the Christian event. For example, for Emmanuel Levinas – and for Derrida, to a certain extent, who takes up and comments on Levinas – there is no real difference between historical times; since every historical moment is immediately related to eternity, the historicity of existence is entirely reduced to its finitude, that is, to the fact that we are *always* already thrown into a situation whose particular traits are given little consideration, compared to the purely 'vertical' relation to the Eternal, to the Other.

If one is to be consistent with the 'antimetaphysical' reasons that, at least in my view, ultimately drive the return of religion in philosophy today, one must acknowledge that tragic Christianity cannot be the outcome of such a return, because it does not accommodate the full meaning of the announcement of kenosis, and thus falls back on a conception of God which not only presents all the traits of the metaphysical God – the 'ultimate', peremptory ground that cannot be transcended – but also explicitly retrieves the personal authority characteristic of the pre-metaphysical God of natural religions.

Reason and the leap

But is not the substance of the Christian faith (God the creator, sin, the necessity of forgiveness and redemption, the resurrection of Christ as the promise of the creatures' final resurrection) so paradoxical as to lend credence to the argument that, once the 'metaphysical' paths to God of Aquinas are recognized as impracticable, the only way of belief left is that of the leap, namely, the readiness to recognize total alterity – which is precisely what is held by tragic and existentialist religiosity? The leap, however, is all the more indispensable the more the words of the gospel are left to their literal sense. What are we to do with a commandment like 'If your eye offends you, pluck it out and throw it away from you?' To be sure, one will reply that even the most committed theoreticians of the paradox-ical leap of faith distinguish between plainly allegorical texts like this and other statements that should be taken literally, such as the historical claims (miracles, the resurrection). This limit – between texts that need 'interpretation' and those that have to be taken literally (a question that remains alive in the whole exegetical tradition) – is always resolved on the basis of the presupposition of a metaphysical rationality that is proclaimed to be natural or, more often, by delegating the decision to the authority of the Church, which has already been accepted by the leap into paradox. Given the premises that have guided me so far, it seems plain to me that it makes no sense to appeal to a natural and self-evident rational background that might establish this distinction; less trivial is the argument concerning the authority of the Church, since I cannot fail to concede that the sacred texts I am referring to, and that I want to interpret, have been passed on to me exclusively by a living tradition, which on this basis can defend the right to teach me how to interpret them.

Here too I am touching on themes that are very controversial in theology and philosophy – I say this exclusively for those who are not familiar with questions concerning hermeneutics and the Catholic catechism. Against the Lutheran principle of the free investigation of Scripture, the Catholic Church sets the thesis that the two sources of revelation are Scripture and tradition. It is a thesis that has always seemed to me preferable to the Protestant 'sola scriptura', because the scriptural text – I am thinking primarily of the New Testament – is itself the crystallization of discourses that were already in circulation in the community of believers. What, in my view, is not acceptable is the idea that the Church's tradition should be infallibly identified with the teaching of Popes and bishops (or rather, in the twentieth century, exclusively by the Pope). By this I mean that the limit represented by the principle of charity, which is to guide the secularizing interpretation of the sacred text, does in fact prescribe that the tradition should be heard charitably; however, what is heard is not confined to the *ex cathedra* teaching of ecclesiastical authority, but is rather the living community of believers. Needless to say, this hearing does not provide clear-cut dogmatic principles like the definitions produced by Popes and councils, which are also themselves to be considered. But the relationship with the living tradition, with the community of believers, is far more personal and risky and is part of the overall duty of giving a personal interpretation of the evangelical message, which is the believer's task.

Accordingly, to hear the words of the gospel, even those that are paradoxical, there is no need for a leap, for what amounts to an irrational acceptance of authority. I am well aware of how important Pascal's thesis of the wager has been

in the history of modern spirituality, in that it has represented the only real alternative so far to the *preambula fidei* of
the Thomistic tradition. Yet one might reflect that Pascal's
wager, the idea that the experience of faith takes the form
of a leap into paradox, is a characteristically *modern* idea that
belongs, broadly speaking, in the epoch of 'triumphalistic'
reason. Pascal was also a mathematician and the theoretician
of the *esprit de géometrie*, and above all the contemporary of
Descartes. And it was no accident that the idea of the
Christian faith as characterized by paradox was taken up by
Kierkegaard, the contemporary of Hegel, in another –
perhaps the last – high point of modern philosophical
rationalism. However, now that Cartesian (and Hegelian)
reason has completed its parabola, it no longer makes sense
to oppose faith and reason so sharply.

What a pity![24]

The gospel is more friendly even towards (late) modern
reason and its demands than an authoritarian conception of
salvation has led us to believe. This friendliness – let me call
it thus on account of God's love for his creatures, which is
the meaning of the biblical message itself – has led me to
adopt the viewpoint of secularization, of weakening, when
looking at many aspects of Christian doctrine which, in
themselves, seem to exclude any friendliness. Christian inter-
locutors, and not just the most orthodox but also those who
do not seem very orthodox but nonetheless incline towards
a tragic or apocalyptic Christianity, always complain that in

---

[24] The Italian expression used by Vattimo here, 'che peccato!' includes a direct
reference to the word sin (*peccato*), which is lost in translation.

the secularized or weak conception of Christianity, the
harshness, severity and rigour characteristic of divine justice
are lost, and with them the very meaning of sin, the actuality
of evil, and as a consequence even the necessity of
redemption.

Of course, it may be an exaggeration to say, as I have
sometimes done in discussions, that, for me, the only Christian meaning of the word 'sin' is an exclamatory one, as in
the expression 'What a pity!' used to convey regret at a lost
opportunity, at a friendship that has ended, and generally
(by extension) at the finitude of everything that has value,
and to which we feel deep attachment. But should we not
acknowledge that Jesus delivers us from sin primarily by
unmasking it in its nullity? Will not the same thing happen
to sin as to the many ritual prescriptions found in the Old
Testament that Jesus set aside as provisional and no longer
necessary? Neither the Sabbath ('Man is not for the Sabbath,
but the Sabbath for man'), nor even circumcision is any
longer an indispensable condition for belonging to the
people of God. What is to keep us from thinking that even
the other sins, which we still believe to be such, are not
destined one day to be unveiled in the same light?

Resistance to this thought is wholly bound up with the
idea that there are sins that may be defined as such on the
basis of natural law, or a metaphysical vision of essences.
This metaphysical vision, however, is just the absolutization
of a historically determined vision of the world, which is
due as much respect (for love of one's neighbour) as any
other cultural production of humanity, but not more. Fine,
one might say, but then will even the commandment 'Do
not kill' be secularized one day? Let me remind you that
charity is the norm of secularization, or more generally, in
the language of ethics, it is the reduction of violence in all
its forms. In view of this limit of charity – which can be
applied not only to murder but, to a certain extent, also to

scandal: it commands a sort of respect for the moral expec-
tations of others, for the community in which I live, which
cannot be overturned at a single stroke solely for the love of
'truth', of which one might claim to be the depository –
Christ's action in relation to evil may be regarded as one of
ironic dissolution: all of which is in stark contrast to much
Christian attitude which feels compelled to exaggerate the
enormous power of evil in the world, as if to emphasize the
saving power of the one who delivers us from it. The Old
Testament, and certain pages of the New Testament, are rife
with situations where divine justice seems to be applied in
frightful ways, often according to the vicious customs of
society at the time.[25]

In the course of the conversation that got this book
started, Sergio Quinzio objected that I cannot put aside
God's righteous face to retain only the loving and merciful
one. Both aspects, he said, are present in the Scriptures, and
the believer must accept them equally. And how is one to
reconcile them? The fact that it is impossible, for us, to
achieve any such reconciliation is an expression of the
terrible and transcendent character of God's enigmatic
nature; once again, there is a demand for a 'leap', an
'acceptance'. Yet is the incomprehensibility of God not
another remnant of the violent prejudices of natural religion
from which Jesus sought to deliver us? Let me add that
although I cannot offer a proof, I have the impression (my
sense is that it is a pervasive impression) that there are fewer
pages in the New Testament regarding 'justice' than 'mercy';
this leads me to my belief that the relation between the two
faces of God in fact constitutes a relation between different
moments of the history of salvation, and that divine justice
is an attribute that is rather close to the natural conception

[25] For example, cf. the terrifying ending of Psalm 137: 'Happy shall he be who takes
your little ones and dashes them against the rock.'

of the sacred, which must be "secularized" precisely in the name of the commandment of love.

However, could God ever cease calling what is unjust by the name of injustice, ever renounce completely his role of judge? Is not religion primarily a thirst and a hunger for justice, seldom realized on this earth, which therefore demands to be reinstituted in eternity by means of a particular judgement (which everybody undergoes at the moment of his or her death) or at the last judgement? If in these judgements we expect God to confine himself to the application of justice, like any human tribunal, though endowed with a perfect balance and infallibility, what shall we make of God's promise to forgive sins? To say, as a way out, that God forgives only those who deserve it – for example, by repenting of everything they have done – would be a rather tawdry solution to the need for a restoration of the broken order: it would, of course, not be enough to satisfy either someone whose family had been destroyed by a murderer, or the survivors of the Holocaust.

God may well be a judge, and yet forgive: this is ultimately the mystery we have to reckon with. And it becomes more intelligible if we recognize that we all stand in need of forgiveness; not because we have broken sacred principles that were metaphysically sanctioned, but rather because we have 'failed' toward those whom we were supposed to love – God himself perhaps (who is not, as we have often been told, identical with the natural law) and the neighbour through whom God becomes present for us.

If we look at the (exclusively) exclamatory meaning of the term 'sin' in this fashion, it is more acceptable and not so far removed from what might be thought in Christian terms. Such a conception of guilt cannot be directly translated into juridical terms. And those who do not want to leave God's justice aside are often preoccupied above all with the earthly order. Of course, the word 'sin' itself has no meaning, according to the laws of the world. The point, however, is not to seek reassurance in the refuge of a sharp distinction between the natural and the supernatural order; for this would be another of those distinctions that in these pages I have proposed we call 'metaphysical' and thus marked by violence.

Secularization concerns not just the substance of Scripture, but also and inseparably the structure and order of the world. With no illusion over natural laws, and solely on the basis of the commandment of charity, Christians move through the world order according to the principles proper to it. They obey the rules of the game and do not presume that their appeal to the 'supernatural' gives them any right to break them. Yet they must also look on this order as a system that needs to become lighter, less punitive, more open to recognize the (sometimes good) reasons of the culprits, in addition to the rights of the victims.

Fine, one might say (among other things): won't this recovery of Christianity be an effort to give power to weak thought, that is, to a particular philosophy, thus legitimating and recommending it as the authentic heir of the prevalent religious tradition which is dominant in Western society? One might be curious to know whether, as Sergio Quinzio asked me in the conversation mentioned above, I believe in the resurrection (of Christ or of all creatures); or more simply, whether I pray, whether I go to Mass. I concede that all these questions are not inspired merely by curiosity about my private life (which I would absolutely reject as futile), but rather by the aim of understanding whether, from my perspective, the link between post-metaphysical thought, weak ontology and nihilism on the one hand, and Christian doctrine on the other, is in the end resolved in favour of one or the other term. Could I really claim to have 'rediscovered' Christianity, if I were to confine myself to the theoretical explanation that weak ontology is the heir of the Christian tradition? Having conceded that it is the heir of Christianity, and that it is made possible by this heritage, is weak thought led to pray to God or Jesus Christ?

I have already said above that if we are to stop thinking of Being in metaphysical terms as a necessary structure given once and for all, it must be conceived as event; this event is the outcome of an initiative, of which I am an 'effect', an heir, an addressee. If, as I believe, religious experience consists in a feeling of dependence (as Schleiermacher rightly defined it), an awareness that my freedom is an initiative that has been initiated by someone else (as Pareyson put it), then the philosophical thought of Being as event is intrinsically oriented toward religion. To be sure, turning to God in prayer entails something more, that is, a conception of the divine as person. I know well enough that there are religious forms of spirituality (Buddhism) where prayer does not imply the existence of something like a divine person to whom one can turn. Accordingly, when I pray – since I pray in the most traditional manner, mainly by reciting the psalms and other prayers of the Roman breviary – I am aware that I am not merely acting on the basis of a philosophical persuasion, but am going a step further. Conversely, it is the philosophical reading I believe I can give of Christianity, focused on the idea of secularization, that itself allows me to avoid any pretension of having completely rationalized my religious attitude: I can accept that many things that I think and say when I pray might undergo a further possible secularization (for example: the idea that God is father, and not mother; or even the idea that God is a person like me). Then, the dissolution of metaphysical reason, of its claim to grasp true Being once and for all, allows me also to accept a measure of 'myth' in my life, which need not necessarily be translated in rational terms – ultimately reason too must be secularized in the name of charity; for example, in the name of the sympathy that I feel towards the Christian tradition, the admiration provoked by (almost all) the virtues of the saints, as I have already mentioned, the feeling I have, in spite of everything, of belonging to the Church, understood as the community of those who believe in Jesus Christ – even, indeed especially, those who pay little attention to the Pope, to his prejudices.

In the end, 'to believe in belief' means a bit of all this: it may be to wager in the sense of Pascal, hoping to win while having no reassurance. To believe in belief, yet also: hoping to believe.

Postscriptum

The manuscript of this small book was ready at the beginning of July 1995, though it was sent to the publisher only in December of the same year. This had less to do with further elaborations and corrections I might have made than with doubts that I held for a long time over the 'legitimacy' of the style I had adopted, which seemed to me, and still seems, too centred on the first person. I have decided to publish it in any case, because I am convinced that a discourse on religion, which is not merely an erudite investigation, whether historical or documentary, can only be formulated in this fashion. The suspicion with which we tend to look at this kind of writing seems to reflect the tendency, which is pervasive in our culture today, to produce religious discourses without taking on the risk of direct and personal engagement in the experiences and matters of which one speaks. This pervasive attitude may be well grounded: for example, a legitimate diffidence towards the 'truth' of subjective experiences, or warranted irony towards those who speak with their hearts on their sleeves, believing that such sincerity justifies the worst trivialities or the most sickening sentimentalism. Yet by the same token, the 'impersonal' tone of many discourses on religion often seems to conceal a kind of moral hypocrisy which should be unmasked or made unacceptable precisely by religious experience. It should have become plain from Kierkegaard's work that we can no longer adopt an impersonal and detached stance towards religious discourse.

Nevertheless, from what I have said briefly and summarily in the preceding pages about Kierkegaard, tragic Christianity, the paradox and the leap, it will be clear that I feel a sort of sympathy towards those who object to the use of overly direct discourse, and who prefer instead – as I do in the case of the liturgy – to speak 'in Latin' of matters of faith, that is, through the screen of rituality, of a language that has been 'monumentalized' by tradition, and which can deter the false truth of lived immediacy. By acknowledging the motives of personal and 'testimonial' involvement, as well as those of detachment and mediation, I am consciously emphasizing the embarrassment I felt in reading this book. There are often passages where the 'I' should have been a 'we', according to the established conventions of discursive essay; elsewhere, the 'we' which has been kept should be read, perhaps, as an 'I'. I wonder whether it will still be possible for me to write essays and 'treatises' in the canonical forms to which I have been used as a philosophical writer: for it is not clear why all that justifies and demands the first person singular in a 'religious' text should not hold, for the same reasons, for a philosophical text. I do not wish to lapse into the narcissism which, in my view, characterizes much philosophical writing that is overly attentive to these kinds of problems: who am I that speaks, who is the 'we' in the name of which I believe to speak, and so on. Yet, in the wake of writing this small book, which is both 'edifying' and autobiographical, I am no longer sure that to pay attention to these questions is to indulge in the narcissism of style instead of entering *in medias res*. After all, even Descartes's *Discourse on Method* (*si licet . . .*) was written in the first person. Accordingly, I am inclined to think that the 'return' of the religious problematic into philosophy, neither by chance nor for stylistic reasons, forces us to revise the mode in which philosophical discourse is formulated, at least in the way I have conceived and practised it.

I do not presume that the reader will be interested in these autobiographical reflections. On the contrary, this postscriptum was inspired by the need to respond to some observations expressed by the first readers, friends to whom I had shown the text during the months that I had let go by before handing the text over to the publisher, owing to the uncertainty over the issue of 'the first person' alluded to above. Most observations revolve around two points: (a) whether it is philologically correct and justified to reduce the theology of 'the wholly other' to a tragicism which merely reproduces the naturalistic conception of divinity as a mysterious and capricious Being impervious to reason (and to any reasonableness), and which in the end can be approached only through blind submission and perhaps magic practice; (b) whether the idea of the Judaeo-Christian revelation as kenosis and the friendliness of God towards his creatures does not give rise to a Christianity that is too optimistic, and which tends to forget the harsh reality of evil – understood less as sin than as inexplicable suffering, as resistance of the 'principle of reality' that continually returns in our experience, against which we can only appeal to the grace of a God who is 'other'.

Beside the question concerning the evaluation of dialectical theology (which, I concede, I have treated too hastily; but I hope to come back to it at another time), these two observations can be reduced to one: whether religion, in the form revealed by Jesus, should not retain the sense of an experience of transcendence which requires a leap, which I have already said that I mistrust. To mistrust the leap seems to signify a refusal to recognize the reality of evil, which contradicts at least the principle of charity itself: perhaps I can endure and secularize evil insofar as it concerns me, but I have to take it seriously when it has to do with the neighbour who calls for my help, or at least for my understanding of his suffering.

In all this, there is certainly a question regarding the *Stimmung*, the spiritual atmosphere in which Christianity is lived. What matters to me is to refuse a Christianity that wants to affirm religion as a necessary way out of an 'intractable' reality. Once again, I am referring to Bonhoeffer's idea of God as the 'stop-gap', according to which reason can only approach God through failure and defeat. It is likely that such an attitude will ultimately lead to an emphasis on the reality of evil, the unsurpassability of human limits, and the idea of history as a place of suffering and trial, rather than as the history of salvation. Thus it would be too easy to level the accusation of indifference to the evil in the world back against those who have formulated the same accusation from the perspective of tragic Christianity; too often in the history of the Church the emphasis on the unsurpassability of the reality of evil through human means has led to an acceptance of all the evil in the world, which is entrusted to the unique action of divine grace. Conversely, through the act of incarnation God, according to all the senses of kenosis, has made possible a historical engagement, conceived less as the acceptance of a trial or as the quest for merits with a view to the beyond, than as the effective realization of salvation.

So I do not believe that the optimism which is bound up with the 'weak' reading of Christian revelation necessarily leads to an undervaluation of the evil in the world. It is true that the tragic position seems to correspond, in many senses, to the apocalyptic experiences that twentieth-century humanity has lived through: the perverse effects of scientific and technological 'progress', the emergence of apparently insoluble existential questions. Yet the 'leap' into transcendence may have at most a sense of consolation; beyond this, it becomes the source of a superstitious – magic and naturalistic – interpretation of the divine. Of course, I do not deny consolation. The Holy Spirit, which Jesus sent at Pentecost and which helps the Church in its secularizing interpretation of Scripture, is also the authentic spirit of consolation. Accordingly, the salvation I seek through a radical acceptance of the meaning of kenosis does not depend exclusively on me, and is not indifferent to the need for grace as the gift that comes from the other. Yet, grace is also characteristic of a harmonious movement that excludes violence, effort, the gnashing of teeth (to use Nietzsche's image) of the dog that has been chained for a long time. The fact that the philosophical kernel of the argument developed here is hermeneutics, that is, the philosophy of interpretation, shows the fidelity of the latter to the idea of grace, understood in its double sense: as a gift that comes from an other, and as a response that inseparably expresses the most intimate truth of the one who receives it in its acceptance of the gift. (Once again, I am referring to the theory of interpretation of Luigi Pareyson, mentioned in the course of the argument.)

One could conclude that the proposal to interpret Scripture by reading the signs of the times is not enough: tragic Christianity, as I have already said, corresponds too closely to the pervasive *Stimmung* of the end of this millennium, which, I believe, must be opposed because it culminates in fundamentalism, the enclosure of oneself within the restricted horizon of communities, the violence which is implicit in the model of the Church as an army that is ready for battle, the inclination to be ill-disposed towards the easing of existence promised, and partly realized, by science and technology. So the idea of reading the signs of the times has an eschatological implication, as in the gospel texts where it appears,[26] which always allude to the last judgement. From the perspective I have illustrated here, this means that in reading the signs there is also a norm which is not entirely reduced to them; the choice between tragicism and secularization can only be made by appealing to the eschatological 'norm'. In my view, this norm – charity – which is destined to remain even when faith and hope will no longer be necessary, when the kingdom of God will be fully realized, justifies completely the preference for a 'friendly' conception of God and of the sense of religion. If this is an excess of tenderness, then it is God who has given us an example of it.

[26] Luke 12: 54ff; Matthew 24: 32ff.